IAIN CRICHTON SMITH writes – 'I was born in 1928. I have written in both Gaelic and English and am a native Gaelic speaker. My aims in my writing are to write about human beings and to compose significant images. I admire, in English, Robert Lowell and Robert Frost and, in Gaelic, as I have been taught to, the great seventeenth century songs. I teach in a large secondary school. I have a number of young student friends whose friendship I treasure because they are, I believe, less hypocritical, more humanly concerned and less priggish that I was at their age.' He won the PEN prize for the best book of poems of 1970.

NORMAN MACCAIG writes – 'Since I am threequarters a Scottish Gael and one quarter a Borderer, it might be expected that my writing would be threequarters cool and classical and one quarter romantic. Whether it is or not, that's what I would like it to be.

   I once had a severe attack of fuzzy-edged, surrealistic verbojuice which I believe I successfully survived (though I still suffer occasionally from whimsy, its fading after-effects). This left me with a strong preference for poetry with hard outlines, with no fat on it, and with a dislike for poetry whose difficulty seems wilful, careless or conning. Yet, I tell myself cautiously, clarity has many modes . . .'

GEORGE MACKAY BROWN was born in Stromness in the Orkneys in 1921 and still lives there. He attended Newbattle Abbey College and read English at Edinburgh University. He is a full-time writer and has published five books of poetry (the latest *Fishermen with Ploughs* came out in 1971), two books of stories, and a book on Orkney. His first novel is due out in 1972: *Greenvoe*. The main influences in his work (he thinks) are Norse sagas, Scottish ballads and the ceremonies of the Catholic Church. The modern writers of fiction he admires most are Thomas Mann, E. M. Forster, and Jorge Luis Borges.

Penguin Modern Poets

21

IAIN CRICHTON SMITH

NORMAN MacCAIG

GEORGE MACKAY BROWN

Penguin Books

Penguin Books Ltd, Harmondsworth, Middlesex, England
Penguin Books Australia Ltd, Ringwood, Victoria, Australia

—

This selection first published 1972
Copyright © Penguin Books Ltd, 1972

—

Made and printed in Great Britain
by Cox & Wyman Ltd,
London, Reading and Fakenham
Set in Monotype Garamond

Contents

CONTENTS

NORMAN MacCAIG

CONTENTS

GEORGE MACKAY BROWN

Acknowledgements

The poems by Iain Crichton Smith, with the exception of 'The White Air of March', which was first published in *Scottish International* and for which we owe grateful thanks to the author, are taken from *Selected Poems*, copyright © Iain Crichton Smith, 1962, 1965, 1969; reprinted by permission of Victor Gollancz Ltd.

The poems by Norman MacCaig, with the exception of 'Incident', 'Among the Talk and the Laughter', 'The Piper in the Dark', 'Bluestocking', 'To Make a Poem', 'Memorial', 'Excuse', 'Centre of Centres', 'Battlefield Near Inverness', 'No Fairy Tale', 'Rock Below Suilven' and 'Ace of Spades', which have not been previously published, and for which we owe grateful thanks to the author, are taken from *Riding Lights*, 1955, *The Sinai Sort*, 1957, *A Common Grace*, 1960, *A Round of Applause*, 1963, *Measures*, 1965, *Surroundings*, 1966, *Rings on a Tree*, 1968, and *A Man in My Position*, 1970, all published by The Hogarth Press, by whose permission the poems are reprinted.

The poems by George Mackay Brown are taken from *The Storm*, 1954, published by the Orkney Press, by whose permission the poems are reprinted, and from *Loaves and Fishes*, 1959, *The Year of the Whale*, 1965, *A Spell for Green Corn*, 1970, *Fishermen with Ploughs*, 1971, and *New Poems*, 1971, all published by The Hogarth Press, by whose permission the poems are reprinted.

IAIN CRICHTON SMITH

Statement by a Responsible Spinster

It was my own kindness brought me here
to an eventless room, bare of ornament.
This is the threshold charity carried me over.
I live here slowly in a permanent

but clement weather. It will do for ever.
A barren bulb creates my firmament.
A sister cries: 'I might have learned to wear
sardonic jewellery and the lineament

of a fine beauty, fateful and austere.
I might have trained my perilous armament
on the learned and ferocious. A lover
would have emerged uniquely from that element.'

I know that for a lie, product of fever.
This is my beginning. Justice meant
that a man or woman who succumbs to fear
should not be married to good merriment.

I inspect justice through a queer air.
Indeed he lacks significant ornament.
Nevertheless he does not laugh or suffer
though, like pity's cruelty, he too is permanent.

And since I was trapped by pity and the clever
duplicities of age, my last emolument
returns, thus late, its flat incurious stare
on my ambiguous love, my only monument.

For the Unknown Seamen of the 1939-45 War Buried in Iona Churchyard

One would like to be able to write something for them
not for the sake of the writing but because
a man should be named in dying as well as living,
in drowning as well as on death-bed, and because
the brain being brain must try to establish laws.

Yet these events are not amenable
to any discipline that we can impose
and are not in the end even imaginable.
What happened was simply this, bad luck for those
who have lain here twelve years in a changing pose.

These things happen and there's no explaining
and to call them 'chosen' might abuse a word.
It is better also not to assume a mourning,
moaning stance. These may have well concurred
in whatever suddenly struck them through the absurd

or maybe meaningful. One simply doesn't
know enough, or understand what came
out of the altering weather in a fashioned
descriptive phrase that was common to each name,
or may have surrounded each like a dear frame.

Best not to make much of it and leave these seamen
in the equally altering acre they now have
inherited from strangers though yet human.
They fell from sea to earth, from grave to grave,
and, griefless now, taught others how to grieve.

Old Woman

And she, being old, fed from a mashed plate
as an old mare might droop across a fence
to the dull pastures of its ignorance.
Her husband held her upright while he prayed

to God who is all-forgiving to send down
some angel somewhere who might land perhaps
in his foreign wings among the gradual crops.
She munched, half dead, blindly searching the spoon.

Outside, the grass was raging. There I sat
imprisoned in my pity and my shame
that men and women having suffered time
should sit in such a place, in such a state

and wished to be away, yes, to be far away
with athletes, heroes, Greeks or Roman men
who pushed their bitter spears into a vein
and would not spend an hour with such decay.

'Pray God,' he said, 'we ask you, God,' he said.
The bowed back was quiet. I saw the teeth
tighten their grip around a delicate death.
And nothing moved within the knotted head

but only a few poor veins as one might see
vague wishless seaweed floating on a tide
of all the salty waters where had died
too many waves to mark two more or three.

Schoolgirl on Speechday in the Open Air

Here in their health and youth they're sitting down
on thick tight grass while bald official men
heavy with sunshine wear a moment's crown
and put it by reluctantly again.

I look at one who lies upon her side
wearing bright yellow for the clasping light.
No ring of shadow has engaged her pride
or wolfed her, fallen, in the circling night.

Her scorn springs out like swords. A smile plays round
her unstained lips as if a joke might spill.
She turns her shining head into that sound
which stumbles downward from low hill to hill.

And then I turn again and see how one
dangles her will from every word he spins
and think how thirty years can fence a man
by what he loses and by what he wins

into a little ground where he can see
the golden landlords, pursed with luck, stride past
and schoolgirls, flashing by, are fat and free
as fish he played for but new men will taste.

And the timed applause which falls from rock to rock
and then to silence is the way he came.
She gathers like necessity her cloak.
The schoolgirl rises – and must do the same.

Sunday Morning Walk

Sunday of wrangling bells – and salt in the air –
I passed the tall black men and their women walking
over the tight-locked streets which were all on fire
with summer ascendant. The seas were talking and talking

as I took my way to the wood where the river ran quiet.
The grass lay windowed in sunlight, the leaves were raging
in furious dying green. The road turned right
round the upstanding castle whose stone, unageing,

marks how a world remains as I, being now
pack of a wandering flesh, take holiday, strolling
far from the churches' declaiming. Health will allow
riots of naiads and nymphs, so wantonly rolling

with me in leaves in woods, thinking how once
Jove took his pleasure of Leda or – splendid embracing –
god would mate with a goddess – rapid the pounce,
fruitful the hot-thighed meeting, no need for unlacing.

And occupied thus, I came where a dead sheep lay
close to a fence, days gone. The flies were hissing and buzzing
out of the boiling eyes, wide open as day.
I stood in the sunlight beside it, watching and musing.

Three crows famished yards off. Live sheep grazed far
from the rotting carcass. The jaw, well-shaved, lay slackly
there on the warm quiet grass. The household air
was busy with buzzing like fever. How quickly, how quickly

the wool was peeled from the back! How still was the flesh!
How the visiting flies would not knock at the door of the
    sockets!

How the hole in the side gaped red, a well-sized gash!
How the clear young lambs grazed in the shade of the
   thickets!

And the sun blazed hot on my shoulder. Here was no shade.
But the sheep was quiet, so quiet. There was nothing to
   notice
but the grape-bunched flies and the crows. Could a world
   have stayed
if I'd taken a stick in my hand to beat off the flies?

They would merely return when I'd gone and busy as always
inhabit this larder again no matter how brightly
I struck with my smart sharp stick. All I could praise –
yes, all I could praise – was the sheep lying there so quietly

not knowing, not knowing. High summer was raging
   around.
I stood in my slack clean clothes. The stones were burning.
The flies in the wound continued their occupied sound
as I turned my back on a death of no weeping or mourning.

IAIN CRICHTON SMITH

Kierkegaard

Forced theologian of the minimum place,
the Copenhagen of the hunchback soul
eclipsed yet strengthened all his natural rays.
Imagine him daily taking his cramped stroll
by sniggering windows to a North Pole
where his wit spawned its cold rainbow oil.

His father was Abraham on a high hill.
The knife cut Isaac to the head and heart.
Ingenious loneliness decorated hell
with books he fathered on a girl's spirit.
She sank her roses into his cold desert
who drove his body deeper into art.

Tragedy? or Comedy? These meet
in the written mirrors furnishing his chill
and flashing Danish room, for all the light
was self-absorbed into that crucial
omnivorous intelligence so cruel
it mocked the pain that made the bare brain howl.

Till the new category, the individual,
rose like a thorn from the one rose he knew.
The crucifixion of the actual
by necessary acceptance brought him through
to where his father, standing calm and new,
cutting his head and life made one from two.

By Ferry to the Island

We crossed by ferry to the bare island
where sheep and cows stared coldly through the wind –
the sea behind us with its silver water,
the silent ferryman standing in the stern
clutching his coat about him like old iron.

We landed from the ferry and went inland
past a small church down to the winding shore
where a white seagull fallen from the failing
chill and ancient daylight lay so pure
and softly breasted that it made more dear

the lesser white around us. There we sat,
sheltered by a rock beside the sea.
Someone made coffee, someone played the fool
in a high rising voice for two hours.
The sea's language was more grave and harsh.

And one sat there whose dress was white and cool.
The fool sparkled his wit that she might hear
new diamonds turning on her naked finger.
What might the sea think or the dull sheep
lifting its head through heavy Sunday sleep?

And later, going home, a moon rising
at the end of a cart-track, minimum of red,
the wind being dark, imperfect cows staring
out of their half-intelligence, and a plough
lying on its side in the cold, raw

naked twilight, there began to move
slowly, like heavy water, in the heart
the image of the gull and of that dress,
both being white and out of the darkness rising
the moon ahead of us with its rusty ring.

Home

To have to stay
in spite of scorn, hatred,
in spite of shattered
illusions also. To be unable
to break cleanly away
since this is truly home
simple, imperishable,
since otherwhere is chill,
dull-breasted, dumb.

Since this too is hated,
loved, willed to be perfect, willed
to a finer yield,
fiercer, less barren, richer,
its harvests be completed.
Since to have seen tall men
moving in light and fire
yet human too is more
grace than can be given

this (one says) is tragic
(to be fixed on a wheel
implacable, internal,
as tears break, as roses
bowed gravely down to rock
proliferate endless versions)
is not tragic but cause
of fresh honours, horses
impelled by used reins.

Deer on the High Hills – A Meditation

I

A deer looks through you to the other side,
and what it is and sees is an inhuman pride.

II

Yesterday three deer stood at the roadside.
It was icy January and there they were
like debutantes on a smooth ballroom floor.

They stared at us out of that French
arrogant atmosphere, like Louis the Sixteenth
sustained in twilight on a marble plinth.

They wore the inhuman look of aristocrats
before a revolution comes, and the people
blaspheme the holy bells in the high steeple.

Before the ice breaks, and heroes in spring
come up like trees with bursting wrongs in their arms
and feed the nobles to the uniform worms.

So were these deer, balanced on delicate logic,
till suddenly they broke from us and went
outraged and sniffing into the dark wind.

Difficult to say where they go to
in the harsh weather when the mountains stand
like judging elders, tall on either hand.

Except that they know the ice is breaking now.
They take to the hills pursued by darkness and lie
beneath the starry metaphysical sky.

Sometimes in a savage winter they'll come down
and beg like fallen nobles for their bread.
They'd rather live in poverty than be dead.

Nevertheless there's something dangerous
in a deer's head. He might suddenly open your belly
with his bitter antlers to the barren sky.

Especially in winter when tormented
by loneliness they descend to this road
with great bounding leaps like the mind of God.

In summer they can be ignored. They crop so gently
among the hills that no one notices
their happy heads sunk in the feeding cresses.

But beware of them now when ice is on the ground.
A beggared noble can conceal a sword
next to his skin for the aimless and abhorred

tyrants who cannot dance but throw stones,
tyrants who can crack the finest bones:
tyrants who do not wear but break most ancient crowns.

III

One would be finished with these practical things
in order to return as deer do
to the tall mountain springs.

Nevertheless one should not so return
till soldier of the practical or doer
one wholly learns to learn

a real contempt, a fine hard-won disdain
for these possessions, marbles of unripe children,
as, again,

a deer might walk along a sweating street
stare in a cramped window and then go
back to the hills but not on ignorant feet.

IV

Forget these purple evenings and these poems
that solved all or took for myth
the pointed sail of Ulysses enigmatic.

There was Hector with his child in his arms.
Where is that other Hector
who wore the internal shield, the inner sword?

Ulysses scurries, like a rat trapped in a maze,
he wears the sharp look of a business magnate.
Late from the office he had a good excuse.

Ideas clash on the mountain tops.
By the appalled peaks the deer roar.
Simply a question of rutting, these cloudy systems

or as yesterday we saw a black cloud
become the expression of a tall mountain.
And that was death, the undertaker, present.

And all became like it for that moment,
assumption of anguish, and the hollow waters
the metaphysics of an empty country

deranged, deranged, a land of rain and stones,
of stones and rain, of the huge barbarous bones,
plucked like a loutish harp their harmonies.

V

You must build from the rain and stones,
from the incurable numbers: the grasses
innumerable on the many hills.

Not to geometry or algebra,
or an inhuman music, but
in the hollow roar of the waterfall,

you must build from there and not be
circumvented by sunlight or a taste of love
or intuitions from the sky above

the deadly rock. Or even history,
Prince Charles in a gay Highland shawl,
or mystery in a black Highland coffin.

You must build from the rain and stones
till you can make
a stylish deer on the high hills,
and let its leaps be unpredictable!

VI

Duncan Ban McIntyre, the poet,
knew them intimately, was one of them.
They had waxen hides, they were delicate dancers.

They evolved their own music which became
his music: they elected him
their poet laureate.

It was a kind of Eden these days
with something Cretan in his eulogy.
Nevertheless he shot them also.

Like shooting an image or a vivid grace.
Brutality and beauty danced together
in a silver air, incorruptible.

And the clean shot did not disturb his poems.
Nor did the deer kneel in a pool of tears.
The stakes were indeed high in that game.

And the rocks did not weep with sentiment.
They were simply there: the deer were simply there.
The witty gun blazed from his knowing hand.

VII

What is the knowledge of the deer?
Is there a philosophy of the hills?
Do their heads peer into the live stars?

Do rumours of death disturb them? They do not live
by local churchyards, hotels or schools.
They inhabit wild systems.

Do they outface winds or lie down
in warm places? Winter, interrogant,
displaces spring and summer, undulant.

Their horns have locked in blood. Yes, their horns
have gored bellies. The dainty hind
has absolute passion, similar and proud.

It is not evil makes the horns bright
but a running natural lustre. The blood
is natural wounding. Metaphoric sword

is not their weapon, but an honest thrust.
Nor does the moon affect their coupling, nor
remonstrant gods schoolmaster their woods.

Evil not intentional, but desire
disturbs to battle. The great spring is how
these savage captains tear to indigo

the fiery guts. Evil's more complex, is
a languaged metaphor, like the mists that scarf
the deadly hind and her bewildered calf.

VIII

Supposing God had a branched head like this
considering Himself in a pool.
It is not the image of the beautiful

makes it so, simply as in a mirror,
but in its fadingness, as on the ice
the deer might suddenly slip, go suddenly under,

their balance being precarious. It is this,
that makes her beautiful, she who now obscures
unconscious heavens with her conscious ray,

is concourse of bright flesh, sad, is remembering
herself so going, so implacable,
her failing voyages to the obstinate rocks:

as deer so stand, precarious, of a style,
half-here, half-there, a half-way lustre breaking
a wise dawn in a chained ocean far.

As dear, so dear, Vesuvius, rocket, you
being ice and water, winter and summer, take
the mountainous seas into your small logic.

God may not be beautiful, but you
suffer a local wound. You bleed to death
from all that's best, your active anima.

The deer and you may well be beautiful,
for through your bones as through a mathematics
concordant honouring beauty richly breaks.

IX

Deer on the high peaks, calling, calling,
you speak of love, love of the mind and body.
Your absolute heads populate the hills

like daring thoughts, half-in, half-out this world,
as a lake might open, and a god peer
into a room where failing darkness glows.

Deer on the high peaks, there have been heads
as proud as yours, destructive, ominous,
of an impetuous language, measureless.

Heads like yours, so scrutinous and still,
yet venomed too with the helpless thrust of spring,
so magisterial, violent, yet composed:

heads of a thirsty intellect, sensuous as
the thirst of bellies in a summer day
July and waspish, on a murmuring ground.

Heads like valleys where the stars fed,
unknown and magical, strange and unassuaged,
the harmonies humming in a green place.

So proud these heads, original, distinct,
they made an air imperial around
their pointed scrutiny, passionate with power.

Electric instinct of the high hills
till, later, later peasants in the valleys
felt in their bones disquieting kingdoms break

and matrons, by small cottages, would sense
implacable navies in their native wombs,
a generation of a harder wit

and later later when the senses quickened
(the hills being bare again) in a new season
in a night honoured with a desperate star

another head appeared, fiercer than these,
disdain flashed from his horns, a strange cry
perplexed the peasants, somnolent, appeased.

X

Deer on the high peaks, the wandering senses
are all, are all: fanatic heads deceive,
like branches springing in a true desert.

Smell now the cresses and the winter root,
passage of heather, journey of rank fox
mortal and moving on the strange hills.

In spring the raven and lascivious swallow,
migrant of air, the endless circle closing,
unclosing, closing, a bewildering ring

of natural marriage, pagan, sensuous.
Return of seasons, and the fugitive
Culloden of scents, erratic, hesitant.

The snow returning, and the summer wasp
more caustic than idea, hum of bees
at their devotions to the wild honey.

The hind crowned with her wanton sex,
rage of the sap in trees, the urgent salmon
pregnant with oceans dying into streams.

And these return in spite of the idea,
the direct reasoning road, the mad Ulysses
so unperverted, so implacable,

so wearing late his dull ironic crown
among a people he has never loved
nor felt in boredom kinship ominous

but fixed on a reasoned star his obstinate gaze
who came at last to where his childhood was
an infant island in an ancient place.

XI

Deer on the high peaks, let me turn
my gaze far from you, where the river winds
its slow way like an old man's argument.

The rocks obstinate, the rains persistent,
the stones ingathered into their chastened fury,
all things themselves, a fierce diversity.

The rampant egos of the flat plains,
the thorns gentle with their sour flowers,
tongues of the sharp stones, the water's business.

Contorted selves that twist in a dark wind,
far from the mountains, from the far and clear
ordered inventions of the stars ongoing.

And here, below, the water's business
smoothing the stone, consenting to the heads
that, easy of a summer, stare and stare

and speak: 'I am, I am. Preserve me, O preserve.
Make me in mirror matchless and the earl
of such imagined kingdoms as endure.

I pray, I pray, a marchioness of this
dismembered kingdom, let my face be seen
not mortal now but of a lasting grace.'

Roar of the waters, prickly thrust of thorn,
immutable stone, sand of a brute fact,
these are the maenads of necessity.

And the deer look down, Platonic dawn breaks
on Highland hills as distant as a thought,
an excellent Athens, obstinate mirage,

while the stone rears, the venomed stone rears
its savage being, and the waters pour
illusive summers to the real seas,

while the deer stand imperious, of a style,
make vibrant music, high and rich and clear,
mean what the plain mismeans, inform a chaos.

XII

Deer on the high hills, in your half-way kingdom,
uneasy in this, uneasy in the other,
but all at ease when earth and sky together

are mixed are mixed, become a royalty
none other knows, neither the migrant birds
nor the beasts chained to their instinctive courses.

That half-way kingdom is your royalty,
you on a meditative truth impaled,
the epicures of feeding absolutes,

you of a metaphysics still and proud,
native to air, native to earth both,
indigenous deer beneath a cloudburst sky:

to whom the lightning's native and the thunder,
whose sockets flash with an annunciant fire,
whose storms are vegetation's dearest friend.

Your antlers flash in light, your speed like thought
is inspiration decorous and assured,
a grace not theological but of

accomplished bodies, sensuous and swift,
of summer scents enjoyers, and of winters
the permanent spirits, watchful, unappeased:

of summer hills a speaking radiance
the body's language, excellent and pure,
discoursing love, free as the wandering wind:

of scentless winters the philosophers,
vigilant always like a tiptoe mind
on peaks of sorrow, brave and scrutinous:

on peaks of sorrow, brave and scrutinous,
on breakneck peaks, coherent and aplomb,
the image silent on the high hill.

XIII

Do colours cry? Does 'black' weep for the dead?
Is green so bridal and is red the flag
and eloquent elegy of a martial sleep?

Are hills 'majestic' and devoted stones
plotting in inner distances our fall?
The mind a sea: and she a Helen who

in budding hours awakens to her new
enchanting empire all the summer day,
the keys of prisons dangling in her hands?

Is night a woman, and the moon a queen
or dowager of grace, and all the stars
archaic courtiers round ambiguous smiles?

Are rivers stories, and are plains their prose?
Are fountains poetry? And are rainbows the
wistful smiles upon a dying face?

And you, the deer, who walk upon the peaks,
are you a world away, a language distant?
Such symbols freeze upon my desolate lips!

XIV

There is no metaphor. The stone is stony.
The deer step out in isolated air.
We move at random on an innocent journey.

The rain is rainy and the sun is sunny.
The flower is flowery and the sea is salty.
My friend himself, himself my enemy.

The deer step out in isolated air.
Not nobles now but of a further journey.
Their flesh is distant as the air is airy.

The rivers torrents, and the grasses many.
The stars are starry, and the night nocturnal.
The fox a tenant of no other skin.

Who brings reports? There's one head to the penny.
A door is wooden, and no window grieves
for lovers turned away, for widows lonely.

The deer step out in isolated air.
The cloud is cloudy and the word is wordy.
Winter is wintry, lonely is your journey.

'You called sir did you?' 'I who was so lonely
would speak with you: would speak to this tall chair,
would fill it chock-full of my melancholy.'

So being lonely I would speak with any
stone or tree or river. Bear my journey,
you endless water, dance with a human joy.

This distance deadly! God or goddess throw me
a rope to landscape, let that hill, so bare,
blossom with grapes, the wine of Italy.

The deer step out in isolated air.
Forgive the distance, let the transient journey
on delicate ice not tragical appear

for stars are starry and the rain is rainy,
the stone is stony, and the sun is sunny,
the deer step out in isolated air.

World War One

I

Haig

These stumbling men (later to be translated
from brutal Flemish into heroic English)
were willed into their last freedom
by this mind, not perhaps stupid,
even, let's say, at first impaled on swords
where blood and glory wept.

But later calmed, not in simple ambition
or Bible's black strength, rather this
public prison walling a private person
where every word meant prevents
the luxury of accident

while these men splashing into roses
through clotting mud, privates mostly,
die into the sentiment of freedom,
and he, clamped to a whirring desk,
(who might have wished that day to be with them)
becomes their deaths, beaten into stone.

2

They droop out of the twilight, slack-rifled,
their eyes tired to stone, their bayonets green.
Around them, an insane loom of light.

A letter winks from a cold pocket.
'Dear Son,' 'Dear Bill.' (A house made of bone
furrows an unmitigated distance.)

Laces trail. This is a sky of heroes
where the small birds are too awed to sing.
Kettles boil in the depths of heads.

Sleepwalking, they pass our tall statues.
Poppies fall on their heads. They don't halt.
They march under the foam of speeches.

As if they're tired. As if they don't see.
Nevertheless their eyes are open.
Strangely in the noise one fixes bayonet,

charges. The blade sinks in wreaths.
He screams onward like a train
through the green pastures of England.

3

Lucky for them that they died perhaps
for now they are not confined to the one ground.
They stride through doors and windows in the moonlight
or stand by altars etched in ideal tears.
Sometimes in woods or among stone fields
they are heard marching, or by humming lawns
where fat men sigh out of their gaping shears
till the music passes: and then return again
to wives, children, bills, the screams of buses.

The dead however can afford to laugh
and crack the old jokes, as they slide their gear
(the hallowed helmet, the wreathed bayonet,
and instant rifle) through those warm mists
and vineyards of a changed France.
Others may die more sourly in slow coffins

hearing the blood creak through old chairs
forgiving daily other worse killings
till secret darkness throttles the red sun –

but these, more free, will neither sag nor frown
nor bear unwilling envy, jealousy,
nor stare like rabbits into the paralysis
of futureless future: for they haven't lived
except as heroes who redeemed the world.
Flares, not quarrels, redden tense faces.
Untidy groceries never weighed them down.
These among others bear our hardest envy
having died into the freedom of their legend.

4

The Soldier's Wish

I want fat cigars to explode
from God's lips. I want the dead
to rise in their hideous truth,
skulls, bones, smells, to writhe
through blind speeches. I want
the full dead to decant
their blood into glasses, at feasts
where the false praisers are guests.
I want the girls who cried 'Heroes'
to be raped by grunts on dead furrows.
And all who spoke without thought
of our 'young warriors' to rot.
In the hushed club papers to blow
their crosswords into stunning snow.
I want it all to come clear –
the wires humming through the air
their loaded corpses: all that mud,

the shocked face, the leaked blood.
I want them to stand, and see.
Let no roses blow over me.
I want them to look down
right to the unsmiling bone.
And lastly I want this:
the skin ripped from a fat face.

5

November 1961

I can't cry for these men.
Their physical wrestling is too strange
for the purer boil that stirs my pen.
They're like the stones of Stonehenge

staggering about blind fields.
The shrill needles of our minds
pierce deeper. There are no shields
either of steel or of diamonds

to jam their craft. Even in the silence
unresting jabbing points hem
a dress composed of violence
and stunned peace. A dry flame

worse perhaps than the physical
burns their untidiness away
from the private to the general
debt that our feelings cannot pay.

6

Here at the droning sermon
this man stands quite clear

as mineral or silver.
The iced bells crash together
like idiot helmets. He
stands stiffly at attention
in a dream without tone.

His face repels inquiry.
Now in the bitter cold
and clear field of memory
he who has grown old
(not like those others) stares
through paper poppies to
more bloody trumpeters.

Not with tears. Not even
with any feeling that
shows on his stopped face.
He could (for whatever thought
cracks upwards through that ice)
be a deserter or
a cool successful surface.

One cannot tell, except
that was a test. His eyes
don't look through the same air
as mine do. More wise?
I let my own eyes drop
to where his boots shine bright
beyond time's appetite

to a fiercer mirror than
any I'll ever know.
His image shook in these.
Mine to my own degrees.

I turn away. He stands
clamped by these Flemish winds.
The bells may give him ease

though none to me. I hear
traffic begin again.
The dizzying cars roar.
Poppies hum in my brain
their senseless wheels. I turn
to where those others burn,
our smaller staggering men,
from jabs of tinier wars.

7

Poppies

Poppies defencelessly bared like hearts
sucked of their green, and all red,
you are the Flanders beyond good
and evil. You've become
not the terror of our art's
untidy whirr, but, I surmise,
aesthetic composed of melodies
where the brute fright stands still
in a Mons of too-sweet miracle.

Old Woman

Your thorned back
heavily under the creel
you steadily stamped the rising daffodil.

Your set mouth
forgives no one, not even God's justice
perpetually drowning law with grace.

Your cold eyes
watched your drunken husband come
unsteadily from Sodom home.

Your grained hands
dandled full and sinful cradles.
You built for your children stone walls.

Your yellow hair
burned slowly in a scarf of grey
wildly falling like the mountain spray.

Finally, you're alone
among the unforgiving brass,
the slow silences, the sinful glass.

Who never learned,
not even ageing, to forgive
our poor journey and our common grave,

while the free daffodils
wave in the valleys and on the hills
the deer look down with their instinctive skills,

and the huge seas
in which your brothers drowned sing slow
over the headland and the peevish crow.

Witches

Coveys of black witches gather
at corners, closes.
Their thin red pointed noses
are in among the mash of scandal.

Poking red fires with
intense breath, hot as the imagined
rape riding the hot mind.
The real one was more moral

and more admirable because animal.
In an empty air they convene
their red, sad, envious beaks. The clean
winter rubs them raw

in a terrible void, hissing
with tongues of winter fire.
Pity them, pity them. Dare
to ring them with your love.

Two Girls Singing

It neither was the words nor yet the tune.
Any tune would have done and any words.
Any listener or no listener at all.

As nightingales in rocks or a child crooning
in its own world of strange awakening
or larks for no reason but themselves.

So on the bus through late November running
by yellow lights tormented, darkness falling,
the two girls sang for miles and miles together

and it wasn't the words or tune. It was the singing.
It was the human sweetness in that yellow,
the unpredicted voices of our kind.

Lenin

In a chair of iron
sits coldly my image of Lenin,
that troubling man
'who never read a book for pleasure alone'.

The germ inside the sealed train
emerged, spread in wind and rain
into new minds in revolution
seeming more real than had been,

for instance, Dostoyevsky. No, I can
romanticize no more that 'head of iron',
'the thought and will unalterably one',
'the word-doer', 'thunderer', 'the stone

rolling through clouds'. Simple to condemn
the unsymmetrical, simple to condone
that which oneself is not. By admiration
purge one's envy of unadult iron

when the true dialectic is to turn
in the infinitely complex, like a chain
we steadily burn through, steadily forge and burn
not to be dismissed in any poem

by admiration for the ruthless man
nor for the saint but for the moving on
into the endlessly various, real, human,
world which is no new era, shining dawn.

IAIN CRICHTON SMITH

At the Firth of Lorne

In the cold orange light we stared across
to Mull and Kerrera and far Tiree.
A setting sun emblazoned your bright knee
to a brilliant gold to match your hair's gold poise.

Nothing had changed: the world was as it was
a million years ago. The slaty stone
slept in its tinged and aboriginal iron.
The sky might flower a little, and the grass

perpetuate its sheep. But from the sea
the bare bleak islands rose, beyond the few
uneasy witticisms we let pursue
their desolate silences. There was no tree

nor other witness to the looks we gave
each other there, inhuman as if tolled
by some huge bell of iron and of gold,
I no great Adam and you no bright Eve.

Envoi

Remember me when you come into your kingdom.
Remember me, beggar of mirrors, when you are confirmed
in the sleep of fulfilment on the white pillow.

Remember me who knock at the window,
who hirple on my collapsing stick, and know
the quivering northern lights of nerves.

Remember me in your good autumn.
I in my plates of frost go
among the falling crockery of hills,

stones, plains, all falling and falling.
In my winter of the sick glass remember
me in your autumn, in your good sleep.

She Teaches Lear

Much to have given up? Martyr, one says?
And to read *Lear* to these condemning ones
in their striped scarves and ties but in the heart
tall, cool and definite. Naval, in this art.
'Brought it on himself. He ran away,
then strained to keep his pomp and circumstance.'

Of course it's true. Much to be said for Regan,
Goneril too. Cordelia just a tune,
and also beautiful as I am not.
'Life must be lived. Life is beyond thought.
These two were living.' Who says that? It's Brown.
The smallest one (with glasses) in the room.

So I go home towards his bitterness,
achieved selfishness, clinging so with claws
to chair and pipe, a dreadful bitter man.
He hates all life, yet lives. Helpless in pain,
trains pain on others. 'Pray,' at night he says,
'undo this button,' and yet hates for this

me out of helplessness. And yet I stay.
'Regan and Goneril had some place to go.'
('Some*where*.' Correct this young American.)
Which side is right? For there is young pale Jean –
she might be one. Responsibility
is weighty, living, in the to-and-fro

of these cool deadly judgements. So she listens,
the true Cordelia, library-white face,
thin-boned and spectacled, speechlessly unhappy,
and ready for all art, especially poetry.

'They had some place to go and pure passions.
The rest's hypocrisy.' Purity of the race?

No, not as far as that. Simply a lie,
to live and feed with one so selfish grown
as age is always selfish. The proud two
spur their tall horses into the bright blue
in search of lust, are willing so to die,
the absolute hunters, Goneril and Regan,

beautiful too with their own spare beauty
when one forgets the haunted piteous fox
(there's always a fox whenever such ride by).
Does Jean, as I do, sniff it? Memory
of dear addictive fences, of the high
tall splendid brutes, past little dreaming flocks.

And yet. . . . More simply. They are what they are,
I am what I am? The sensitive eye
broods by packed windows of interior pain
fastened to writhings, knowing rages mean
often unhappiness, that old men wear
their stubborn angers out of dignity,

the failing vigour – eyes, arms, knees.
Gravity pulls them down into the ground.
Last anger blossoms on its final lip.
'Lear is a child,' I hear. Is this the deep
Greek brilliant irony? I find my peace
in this dictator because I have no kind

child to nourish. No, it's not quite that.
'We'll come to this,' I cry. 'No,' Moira says,
quite definite and calm. 'If I should come

to such a state let all drive me from home.'
Easy enough, I think (but hold the thought)
to speak such words when interested praise

makes your face happy at the Saturday
school-club dance, in yellow, and a hand
glides down your bare arm, it seems, forever.
Why should I speak this loud, my own fever?
And then I know it's right as far's mind may
(without sly falsity) seek to understand.

'It's just in case,' I say, 'in case, malformed' –
(how vulnerable ties and scarves, how pure!)
'by living we are made. It's just in case' –
the need, the need! – Polite and curious
they know of no such need (but Jean). Not armed
nor yet disarmed they sit. Sure or unsure

it hasn't touched them yet, the fear of age.
Regan and Goneril seem more natural.
From our own weakness only are we kind.
Admire such ones but know in your own mind
how they would bring upon us innocent carnage,
the end of Lear, and *Lear,* their own worse will.

At the Sale

Old beds, old chairs, old mattresses, old books,
old pictures of coiffed women, hatted men,
ministers with clamped lips and flowing beards,
a Duke in his Highland den,
and, scattered among these, old copper fire-guards,
stone water-bottles, stoves and shepherds' crooks.

How much goes out of fashion and how soon!
The double-columned leather-covered tomes
recall those praying Covenanters still
adamant against Rome's
adamant empire. Every article
is soaked in time and dust and sweat and rust. What tune

warbled from that phonograph? Who played
that gap-toothed dumb piano? Who once moved
with that white chamber pot through an ancient room?
And who was it that loved
to see her own reflection in the gloom
of that webbed mirror? And who was it that prayed

holding that Bible in her fading hands?
The auctioneer's quick eyes swoop on a glance,
a half-seen movement. In the inner ring
a boy in serious stance
holds up a fan, a piece of curtaining,
an hour-glass with its trickle of old sand.

We walk around and find an old machine.
On one side pump, on another turn a wheel.
But nothing happens. What's this object for?

Imagine how we will
endlessly pump and turn for forty years
and then receive a pension, smart and clean,

climbing a dais to such loud applause
as shakes the hall for toiling without fail
at this strange nameless gadget, pumping, turning,
each day oiling the wheel
with zeal and eagerness and freshness burning
in a happy country of anonymous laws,

while the ghostly hands are clapping and the chairs
grow older as we look, the pictures fade,
the stone is changed to rubber, and the wheel
elaborates its rayed
brilliance and complexity and we feel
the spade become a scoop, cropping the grass,

and the flesh itself becomes unnecessary.
O hold me, love, in this appalling place.
Let your hand stay me by this mattress here
and this tall ruined glass,
by this dismembered radio, this queer
machine that waits and has no history.

By the Sea

I

Sitting here by the foreshore day after day
on the Bed and Breakfast routine

I cower in green shelters, watch the sea
bubble in brown sea-pools, watch the sea

climb to the horizon and fall back
rich with its silver coins, its glittering.

Warmly scarfed, I almost remember how
beggars were, and in the thirties men

jumped from the wheel. I lock my will
on the National Health Service, will not fall

too deep for rescue but for the mind, the mind.
Two clouds loom together and are joined

as are two lovers in their nylon wings,
a yellow flutter on cramped bench. Thick rings

of routine save us, rings like marriage rings.
The yachts seem free in their majestic goings

and the great ships at rest. Helmeted girls
emerge from salons with their golden curls.

2

At Helensburgh the tide is out again –
Famous for no one but John Logie Baird
who stares with hollow vision from his soured
bust in the Gardens, given over to bowls
and large fat flowers, as vulgar as the girls
who holiday on pop and fish-and-chips.
The faded gentry turn their telescopes
on the grey Empire ships. The *Advertiser*
genteely mourns the century of the razor
and evenings on the benches tête-à-tête
the officer-like ladies with their net
handbags illuminated by the Fair's coarse lights
and cheap rotating toy world chew the sights
over and over as the mile from Rhu
shades to a ghastly colour, TV blue.

3

These hundred-year-olds preserved in glazed
skin like late apples. Where the yacht's guns blaze
they're startled in their shelters. Past MacNair –
Celtic's pre First War full back – they can share
tales of long-shirted footballers, rotate
on a fabulous bitten park. O the huge weight
of time's dead failures. (What would you say my age . . .
What would you say my age was?) Pipers wage
a mimic war. Eight and two drummers seem
a hired-out autumn at the minimum
cost to the town. These centenarians know
each blade of grass, each veer of yacht, each slow
seepage of the tide. God's ancient spies
and vultures of the spirit they surprise
by the teeth's grip on meat, persistent fangs
which have outanchored wives, their busy goings.

4

In the Café

The leaf-fringed fountain
with the grey Scots cherub
arches water
over the waterlogged pennies.

Mouths and moustaches move.
The sad-eyed waitress
hides her unringed hand.
Umbrellas stand at ease.

Outside, rain drips
soupily, 'the soup of the day'.
The sauce bottles are filled with old blood
above the off-white linen.

('Not that I didn't have
suitors,' said the Edinburgh lady
seated in the shelter like a queen,
gloved hands on her worn sceptre.)

But the waitress meltingly watches
that white-haired three-year-old,
a huge bubble with wicked teeth
combing his hair with his knife.

5

Milk jugs, cups,
pastries with pink ice,
menus rotating through one meal,
Most of what we do is refuel,
then head for stations, lost in driving rain.

Waitresses with frilly aprons,
I can tell you
how the teeth rot under the pink ice,
and the sky-blue ashtrays contain
a little fire with lipstick, a little fire.

So few are beautiful,
so few outwear the rainy
sag of a dull air, so few ride
naturally as in woodland, the dream
of the eternally cantering proud horses.

Everything drips, drips, drips,
the water, blood, adulterated milk.
The stalls advertise 'Condensed Books'.
All week I have fed on cheap paper
turning like logged swing doors.

6

Dumbarton

They're pulling down the Bingo hall today.
Crash! Through the glass the pole breaks to the walls
of the converted picture house. The stalls
and ornate balcony (once so outré
with its cheap cherubs of the Music Halls,
Victorian children, plump and neatly gay)
crack in white plaster on white overalls.

Where it once stood, a new smooth road will curve
to a late-night bar, pink with its lights and gin.
There will be leather seats, corners for love,
and the newly-learned cuisine
for the European progeny of those grave
unshaven unemployables who spun

one butt-end out, a river-side conclave

spitting in dirty water: who could get
their Marxist heaven from the plush back-row
watching the jerky stars in scratchy light,
who then would in soft twilight rise and go
half-swimming to the park and there would sit
eating their oily chips, the to-and-fro
of hard tall collars cutting at their throats.

7

Out of the grey the white waves mouth at the shore.
This is their day as yesterday it was mine.
Waves, you would drown me. I know it well. The shine
of your naked grins is dangerous, from what core

of unimaginable cold and dark it flashes
pure power from impure salt, the bodies broken
into a frightening Mass, where no words are spoken
but energy turns on its transformer, gnashes

at the very light and stones. I put it down –
this primer on Nuclear Weapons–Science Series –
complete with diagrams and watch the furious
toppling of the grooved and waste-filled dustbin

with the fused bulb, the soggy *Glasgow Herald,*
the ice-cream carton, empty golden pack
of Benson and Hedges, and the silver track
as of a fish swimming in that drowned field.

8

After the Gale

The stunned world stops on its axis.
Slowly the clouds venture out.
The hills steady.

O Rome, duty was not enough –
the fixed spear, the savage mask for farmers,
the sentry in his place.

The upright eaten by the circular
spin of the stormy world, Hades uprooted
by a bright removal van,

the gods turned to pictures on the carnival
rotating with its fixed masks, its wolves
still upright in their chairs.

9

Young Girl

Nothing more impermanent, it appears,
in your bare nylons twittering. The harsh

waves will not overwhelm you as you rock
on tottering heels towards the yellow clock

high on the windy pier. You toughly peck
at your oiled bag of chips, as seagulls break

herring heads like egg-shells, with bulb eyes.
I watch you in your sheer indomitableness

click the late street past yellow café light,
an H.M.S. that's joining the grey fleet.

10

Dunoon and the Holy Loch

The huge sea widens from us, mile on mile.
Kenneth MacKellar sings from the domed pier.
A tinker piper plays a ragged tune
on ragged pipes. He tramps under a moon
which rises like the dollar. Think how here

missiles like sugar rocks are all incised
with Alabaman Homer. These defend
the clattering tills, the taxis, thin pale girls
who wear at evening their Woolworth pearls
and from dewed railings gaze at the world's end.

11

Tourist Driver

He tells us there's a cow and there's a cow.
He names a hill for us and there it is.
I dream a little, rocking towards Hades
on my third spy story, and imagine how,
gloved and helmeted among the lilies,

he might be telling us of Achilles next
and pointing out his cairn with the bruised heel
or Orpheus perhaps becoming real:
and from that quay – how well he knows his text –
old Charon pulling west each half-crown soul.

12

In the Park

Over the shoes in pebbles I sit here.
Behind me, the silent bells of those red flowers.
Under that winged structure Greeks might wander,
retired Achilles in the varying shade

drifted from the Home, telling of wars,
and Helen's mouth open like that soft bloom
which turns to the sun softly in the dew
and busy orbit of the striped wasp.

On the smooth lawn a cat pursues a bird,
great Disney fool. The bird looks at him, flies,
lands and flies and this time doesn't stop.
The cat slouches back among the trees.

A lot of marble, messages in flowers –
this is Barnardo's Year – the door is open
to orphans ejected from our Welfare State,
that cosy bubble with few images.

The marble and carnations of Elysium.
Columns of lilies drink at the warm water.
All day the furious sun scans the lawns
and fat loud Ajax's waddling up to bowl.

13

Days when the world seems like an old French film
or like the old French General Alors
who waves his soldiers into the Foreign Legion.

Days when everyone has a false moustache
and like a clown one kicks the buildings down
in cycles of raw sparks.

Days when it's hard to follow what is said,
fragments of verbs, verbs in a high wind,
French thick-voiced cannonade.

Days when the rain drums steadily on the attic
where once we turned the green leaves of books
under the farmhouse rafters.

Days, days, days. . . . O the French General
standing in the truck with his drum-shaped soldier's hat
waving us towards nothing.

14

At the Silent Films

O Chaplin with your little black moustache,
your twitching lip, your dead-white dummy's face,
your pliant bourgeois cane.

And Valentino – sheikh of the lovely dead –
jerking through the screen's minute sand
on your crumbling marvellous horse.

And all these visual comics, collapsed chairs,
candid pie-filled faces, fluid houses,
and trains without their rails.

And the jerky dead in jerky chariots
with the blunt bucking swords and thorny helmets,
the overquick salute.

All have crumbled into the screen's sands,
Under the piano's bouncing music
they drown and drown and drown,

twittering like the early birds of spring
testing their wings. By the rackety machine
in flash-light they're devoured.

IAIN CRICHTON SMITH

So many dead. So many stars sunk
in the absurd cloud of their furs
in their busy struts and strides.

O happy visual simplicities
elastic huge moustaches, snaky stairs,
hosepipes of comic water.

You still survive, though dead, in all your white.
The sand has not devoured you, lovely teeth.

I see your blizzard smiles.

Jean Brodie's Children

Jean Brodie's children in your small green caps,
I hear you twitter down the avenues.

The great round bells ring out, the Mademoiselle
despairs of English. In the rustling dorms
you giggle under sheets.

'Dear Edinburgh, how I remember you,
your winter cakes and tea, your bright red fire,
your swirling cloaks and clouds.

Your grammar and your Greek, the hush of leaves,
No Orchids for Miss Blandish with a torch
beneath the tweedy blanket.

Ah, those beautiful days, all green and shady,
our black and pleated skirts, our woollen stockings,
our ties of a calm mauve.

Mistresses, iron in their certainty,
their language unambiguous but their lives
trembling on grey boughs.'

If You Are About to Die Now

If you are about to die now
there is nothing I can write for you.
History is silent about this.
Even Napoleon, face huge as a plate,
disguised the advance guard and said:
'Why they sent for my brother is because
he, and not I, is in trouble.'

The screens come down. The nurses disappear
like the tails of fishes. The clouds
are white as cotton wool and also
Dettol outlives the perfume.
The unshaven man in the next ward
is given Shaving Lotion for Christmas.
Sorrow stands like a stork on one leg,
brooding.

The coloured windows give way to plain.
The horsemen crossing the moor are comrades
going the other way into the country
of the undisciplined and the free.
Here there is the Land of the Straight Lines
with a banner black and silent,
a black mirror
with the image of an old rose.

History does not warn us of this.
Napoleon's face expands to a window.
The manic thoughts fly outwards, beating.
'The documents did not tell me.
There was no announcement in the salon.
Why is it that the chairs are getting crooked?

Why is it that my army does not hear me?
They are eating, laughing by the stream.

I shout to them, "Put on your armour."
But they do not listen.
They do not know me, they are relapsing
into the marsh of their idleness.
They are schoolboys escaped from Latin.
O how afraid they are of Excellence.
They admire their faces in the water.

They splash in the new bubbles.'

The White Air of March

I

This is the land God gave to Andy Stewart –
      we have our inheritance.
There shall be no ardour, there shall be indifference.
There shall not be excellence, there shall be the average.
We shall be the intrepid hunters of golf balls.

Have you not known, have you not heard, has it not been
    reported
that Mrs Macdonald has given an hour-long lecture on Islay
and at the conclusion was presented with a bouquet of
    flowers
by Marjory, aged five?
                  Have you not noted
the photograph of the whist drive, skeleton hands,
rings on skeleton fingers?
                  Have you not seen
the glossy weddings in the glossy pages,
champagne and a 'shared joke'.
                    Do you not see
the Music Hall's still alive here in the North? and on the
    stage
the yellow gorse is growing.
                     'Tragedy,' said Walpole, 'for
                          those who feel.
For those who think, it's comic.'
                  Pity then those who feel
and, as for the Scottish Soldier, off to the wars!
The Cuillins stand and will forever stand.
Their streams scream in the moonlight.

2

The Cuillins tower
clear and white.
In the crevices the Gaelic bluebells flower.

(Eastward
Culloden
where the sun shone
on the feeding raven.
Let it be forgotten!)

The Cuillins tower
scale on scale.
The music of the imagination must be restored,
upward.

(The little Highland dancer
in white shirt green kilt
regards her toe
arms akimbo.
Avoids the swords.)

To avoid the sword
is death.
        To walk the ward
of Dettol, loss of will,
where old men watch the wall,
eyes in a black wheel,
and the nurse in a starched dress
changes the air.

The Cuillins tower
tall and white.
March breeds white sails.

The eagle soars.
On the highest peaks
The sharpest axe.

3

Scottish dance music.
                    Wagner.
'The Hen's March to the Midden.'

Sudden,
        the freshening,
the blue wave that will not be drowned.
The green knife from a café.

The four-walled pibroch is too solid.
Quickness! Fish-leap! Incompleteness!

The flash
          that is seen
                      and gone!

Rain-flash
          almost.

(Scottish dance music.
                  Used as torture
to make them confess,
                    the prisoners.)

Outside the adobe,
                  the Hen's March to the Midden.

And all shall be well,
                    unbidden,
the dancers go under the hill.

4

She came one night
                    and she said:
'I've written a small book
on the viola
                    to be printed in London
not at my own expense
                    I hasten to tell you.

And little songs
            I've also written
for a competition
                    in Eurovision.
I tried to get an introduction
but he was too busy
                    surrounded by the flowers
                    – the lion
smiling among the glasses.

Thirty copies have been sold.
            Do you have any contacts
for such texts?
            To break into the light's centre
where the real people are is not easy,
such fakes surround them.
                            To enter,
to enter the light.'

Her hands crossed on her lap,
dazzled.
        Her eyes sparkling.

There will always be hope.

5

March, and the sails fly seaward
                    whiter, whiter.
He bends in the garden, digs his green lawn.
The soil is broken by a busy convocation
of worms, airless undulation.
At midnight they dance on the lawn,
a vivid exercise, a tortuous process.
                    The hedge buds,
puts out white flowers.
                    The sails fly seaward,
the rocks attend the keel.

                    He bends in his garden
under the council house's wide panes
which show this pastoral scene, another house,
and the blue sky of TV.
The exiles have departed,
                    carrying with them
on a green dollar
                    'a country of the heart'.

At midnight the worms dance on the lawn
transforming recreating
                    altering.
The endless process of the roses brings
summer to wandering tourists.

                    The sails
          fly
               seaward.

6

Sundays.
            The great bells toll.
'Let us meet. Let us draw sustenance from each other.'
Let us put aside the *Observer*, let us remember
            the invocations of the *Sunday Post*.
Let our dirty jokes be told in secret
to a small circle of friends.
                        But otherwise
let us make a stand.

The polished tombstones are like mirrors.
Granite. There let us see our reflections.
And, in the silence, listen to the dead growing,
pink hymn books in their hands.

Otherwise let us make a stand
                against permissiveness. If we are quoted
Say 'The Country' say 'Society'
            but
in smoking rooms let not our jokes be counted against us.

Distant, the white sails.

7

(I speak now of those who told the truth.
Let them be praised.
                Dostoyevsky, Nietzsche, Kierkegaard,
Kafka – let them be honoured.
For them there shall be a cross pointing both ways.
Vertical horizontal.
The Idiot waits for the Cossacks in crystal and iron.
The hunchback squeezes the last ounce out of the wine.

Someone climbs to a castle which doesn't exist.
All shall be on trial to a deaf sheriff
and the police stand in their diced caps, so youthful,
the radiance of our law,
Over the steppes the drumming thunder of legions.
They beat on the Cross, the Either Or of his passion
                  the ring falls from his finger.
The drums beat. Who shall welcome the drummers?
At a table of crystal and linen, glitter and water,
the minister blesses their steel.)

8

The exiles have departed,
                leaving old houses.
The Wind wanders like an old man who has lost his mind
'What do you want?' asks the wind. 'Why are you crying?
Are those your tears or the rain?'
I do not know. I touch my cheek. It is wet.
I think it must be the rain.

It is bitter
to be an exile in one's own land.
It is bitter
to walk among strangers
when the strangers are in one's own land.
It is bitter
to dip a pen in continuous water
to write poems of exile
in a verse without honour or style.

9

    There have been so many
    exiles.
        Jews

turn on their limited space
like cows.
            So many
faces blank as watches
telling
        nothing but time.

How can you drink a cup of wine
without tasting the vinegar
without feeling the thorn?

On the high far
Cuillins
I see them climb.

10

What, out of this place,
rises
out of this
scarred ground
fought over and over
endlessly confined,
refined?

Beautiful ghost,
do you put on body,
do you cry?
It is good if you can,
if from your eyes,
bulbs, there should rise
dew,
out of that face
beaten over and over
water,
tears,
refreshment out of your eyes.

11

They died
in a tight ring
around their king.

The ravens squawk over the fresh bodies
peck through the chain mail
as through small windows.

To the end in a hard place among stones
in the cold twilight they parried.

There shall be no withdrawal.
For honour, for something, they fought.
For the silks of the ladies
for the honour of their own arms.

Silver and gold. There was cold silver.
He lies there eaten by the ravens
who peck in the dark, nodding
their heads like small machines.

In the north there is much wailing.
There is fresh dew on the ballads.
In the morning the wells of their eyes are dry.

Remains this –
the honour.

12

The tall buses pass by.
The cottages trail their roses.

Look at the witch at the waterfall.
She does Bed and Breakfast.

'Ah, Freedom is a noble thing.'

Around the Cuillins
the clouds drift like green dollars.

13

I speak (with a little water) of the family of the MacMurrows.
They are a sept of the MacMorris and had good bards
  enough.
They were the repositories of much harp music,
of history, of genealogy.
Much lore did they preserve, much more than we deserve.
Their ruminations are contained in the 'Book of the
  MacMurrows',
'The Annals of the MacMurrows' and much matter
  significant for scholarship
including the first use of the ablative absolute in a
  categorical mode
with animadversions upon the umlaut, the Dawn of the
  Present Participle
though in one or two places the record is unfortunately
  blank.
(With a drink of water) I am prepared to discourse to you
on their relationship to the Mabinogion.
I am willing to unearth their periphrases, to clarify their
  apostrophes
to investigate their commas and propose their periods
but enough I think has been said to show their importance
to the quality of our civilization, our language, and the
  perpetuation
of our culture, our literature and, if I may say so, our Cause.

14

McGonagall
                    why do I see you as a sign?
Why does your drama perplex me?
Endlessly you toil towards Balmoral
to the old lady knitting her slow empire.

Baffled, beaten, buffeted, scorned, despised,
You played 'Macbeth' to a theatre of villains.
You swung your sly cloak through gaslight
a devotee of Art.

All that you wrote is bad, let us agree.
Who would say that Athens is Dundee?
Or the Tay Bridge our Scots Thermopylae?

(At the 'hot gates'
a wreath for heroes.)

And yet how many more have written worse.
Why such a hatred for your bad verse
when every day we see our literature
weakened by loss of passion, loss of power?

Why should you suffer the anonymous
theses and poor parodies of those
whose competence is just as small as yours –
when they unlike you don't even love verse!

Except that they see mirrored in you their own
impenetrable dullness.
                    On her throne
Victoria sits, a 'poetess' indeed
able to beat a poet on the head

who for endeavour should at least receive
an Order more deserved than some who live
in such hypocrisy as will not be
honoured by Athens, and let's hope, Dundee.

15

The Cuillins tower high in the air –
                              Excellence.
We climb from pain to perfume:
the body opens out; gullies,
crevices, reveal the orchis.
The soul flies skyward,
impregnated with scent.
On the right hand
    the sun will tenant
Skye.
        The mist dissipates.
Gold grows at our feet.

16
        Excellence!
'costing not less than everything'
Illusion after illusion dies.
After the gay green, the blackness.
Snatches
'and I mysel in crammasie'.
Rainbows
out of the darkness.
Green,
green moments
or out of the waterfall
a sudden face –
so dearly known and killed.
Minotaur of guilt

coiled at the centre, vivid.
Flashes.
Blades.
Rotors of Glasgow knives.
Irises
held over tenements
intent, inventing,
Periphrases,
white deer stepping by Loch Lomond side.
The dead bury their dead.
The machines finished
underground.

In the white air of March
a new mind.

NORMAN MacCAIG

Summer Farm

Straws like tame lightnings lie about the grass
And hang zigzag on hedges. Green as glass
The water in the horsetrough shines.
Nine ducks go wobbling by in two straight lines.

A hen stares at nothing with one eye,
Then picks it up. Out of an empty sky
A swallow flies and, flickering through
The barn, dives up again into the dizzy blue.

I lie, not thinking, in the cool, soft grass,
Afraid of where a thought might take me – as
This grasshopper with plated face
Unfolds his legs and finds himself in space.

Self under self, a pile of selves I stand
Threaded on time, and with metaphysic hand
Lift the farm like a lid and see
Farm within farm and, in the centre, me.

Culag Pier

A moderate jargon – winches, cries in Gaelic,
Cordage against the sky: most moderate when
A gull slews in with icefloes in his eyes
And a seal of crimson dapper on his beak;
A frosty distance follows where he flies.

Yet see him, pick-and-run, as he hauls a herring
Through slats of a fishbox, ululating oaths
In a sort of Eskimo at whatever stands
Between his greed and his belly – see him swerving
Out of infinity, steered by guts and glands.

The moderate jargon takes the two things in –
The winged etcetera in his etcetera wastes
Or small town gangster pillaging a slum –
And, puffing incense of brine and oily iron,
Jubilates briskly of its kingdom come.

The moderation is, of course, no mask.
Grace is hilarity; and this scene has
Good nature, in two meanings, as its meaning,
Where a transcendence feeds on guts and makes
No bones of it, nor thinks it worth the screening.

And the observing mind, in its own sun,
Takes it as so. Bright baskets swing between
The darkness and the light and herrings go
Where they could not have guessed in their broad ocean,
And ropes seem tangled, but they are not so.

Feeding Ducks

One duck stood on my toes.
The others made watery rushes after bread
Thrown by my momentary hand; instead,
She stood duck-still and got far more than those.

An invisible drone boomed by
With a beetle in it; the neighbour's yearning bull
Bugled across five fields. And an evening full
Of other evenings quietly began to die.

And my everlasting hand
Dropped on my hypocrite duck her grace of bread.
And I thought, 'The first to be fattened, the first to be dead.'
Till my gestures enlarged, wide over the darkening land.

Celtic Cross

The implicated generations made
This symbol of their lives, a stone made light
By what is carved on it.
                              The plaiting masks,
But not with involutions of a shade,
What a stone says and what a stone cross asks.

Something that is not mirrored by nor trapped
In webs of water or bag-nets of cloud;
The tangled mesh of weed
                              lets it go by.
Only men's minds could ever have unmapped
Into abstraction such a territory.

No green bay going yellow over sand
Is written on by winds to tell a tale
Of death-dishevelled gull
                              or heron, stiff
As a cruel clerk with gaunt writs in his hand
– Or even of light, that makes its depths a cliff.

Singing responses order otherwise.
The tangled generations ravelled out
In links of song whose sweet
                              strong choruses
Are those stone involutions to the eyes
Given to the ear in abstract vocables.

The stone remains, and the cross, to let us know
Their unjust, hard demands, as symbols do.
But on them twine and grow
                              beneath the dove
Serpents of wisdom whose cool statements show
Such understanding that it seems like love.

So Many Summers

Beside one loch, a hind's neat skeleton,
Beside another, a boat pulled high and dry:
Two neat geometries drawn in the weather:
Two things already dead and still to die.

I passed them every summer, rod in hand,
Skirting the bright blue or the spitting gray,
And, every summer, saw how the bleached timbers
Gaped wider and the neat ribs fell away.

Time adds one malice to another one –
Now you'd look very close before you knew
If it's the boat that ran, the hind went sailing.
So many summers, and I have lived them too.

Golden Calf

If all the answer's to be the Sinai sort,
The incorruptible lava of the Word
Made alphabetic in a stormspout, what
Mere human vocables you've ever heard,
Poor golden calf, could overbear, I wonder,
   The magniloquence of thunder?

You're for another flame. The Moses in me
Looks with a stone face on our gaudy lives.
His fingers, scorched with godhead, point, and loose
An influence of categorical negatives
That make an image of love, a trope of lover.
   Our dancing days are over.

The buckles tarnish at the thought of it.
The winecup shatters. The bragging music chokes
To the funeral silence it was awkward in.
And before the faggot of salvation smokes,
Your knees are loosed, your wreathed neck bows lowly
   In presence of the holy.

What's a disgruntled cloud to you or me?
Listen to my multitudes and beam for them,
Making a plinth of this dark wilderness.
Utter such rigmaroles an apothegm,
Doing its head-stroke, drowns in such wild water
   And proves itself no matter.

Or where's the desert cat or hunching shade
That ambles hugely in the dark outside
Or hospitable anguish beckoning

To its foul ceremony a sorry bride
Could bear the darts struck from your hide by torches
   That guard our pleasure's marches?

Forty years. Small wilderness to unravel
Such an unknotted thread of wandering.
The desert is in Moses' skull, the journey
To the white thalamus whose cradling
Enfolds the foetus of the Law – gestation
   Of Moses as a nation.

A chosen people, since they have no choice.
The doors are locked, the fleshpots on the shelves,
And a long line of lamentation moves
Led by the nose through their own better selves
To buy with blood a land of milk and honey
   Where's no need for such money.

The smoke and thunder die. And here I stand
Smelling of gunpowder and holiness.
The great fire does its belly-dance and in it
You shine unharmed, not knowing what's to confess;
And the desert, seeing the issue grows no clearer,
   Takes one long slow step nearer.

Standing in My Ideas

Never did Nature, that vogue-mistress, give
An image from her slants and sighs and silks
Or make a figure out of froth and stone
That would not blush as your alternative
– Though, trapped in a net of kins, a web of ilks,
The gorgeous rose is sibling to the bone.

You stand entrancing in my trance of woods,
Superlatively you; and bole and bough
Surrender Ariels rotting in their rind.
The dropped cone hiccups, the cherry branch intrudes.
And with such grace you breathe what, I allow,
Is foxglove vapours hazing in my mind.

Such elegant composure I suspect
Because I love it, and my loving charms
Environment from you. And, being wise
In my suspicions, can it be I detect
Something of innocent ivy in your arms?
Something of nightshade in those lucid eyes?

Basking Shark

To stub an oar on a rock where none should be,
To have it rise with a slounge out of the sea,
Is a thing that happened once (too often) to me.

But not too often – though enough. I count as gain
That once I met, on a sea tin-tacked with rain,
That roomsized monster with a matchbox brain.

He displaced more than water. He shoggled me
Centuries back – this decadent townee
Shook on a wrong branch of his family tree.

Swish up the dirt and, when it settles, a spring
Is all the clearer. I saw me, in one fling,
Emerging from the slime of everything.

So who's the monster? The thought made me grow pale
For twenty seconds while, sail after sail,
The tall fin slid away and then the tail.

Sheep Dipping

The sea goes flick-flack or the light does. When
John chucks the ewe in, she splays up two wings
That beat once and are water once again.

Pushing her nose, she trots slow-motion through
The glassy green. The others bleat and plunge –
If she must do it, what else is there to do?

They leap from ledges, all legs in the air
All furbelows and bulged eyes in the green
Turned suds, turned soda with the plumping there.

They haul themselves ashore. With outraged cries
They waterfall uphill, spread out and stand
Dribbling salt water into flowers' eyes.

Fishing the Balvaig

It is like being divided, stood on stumps
On a layer of water scarcely thicker than light
That parallels away to show it's water all right.

While underneath two sawn-off waders walk
Surprisingly to one's wishes – as though no man
Moved lumpishly, so, but a sort of Caliban.

The eel that tries to screw his ignorant head
Under an instep thinks the same; and goes
Like a tape of water going where the water flows.

Collecting images by redounding them
The stream is leafed, sunned, skied and full of shade:
Pot-holed with beer and shallowed with lemonade.

But in the glides is this thicker sort of light.
It blurs no freckled pebble or nervous weed,
Whose colours quicken as it slacks its speed,

As though water and light were mistranslations of
A vivifying influence they both use
To make a thing more thing and old news, news.

Which all the world is, wheeling round this odd
Divided figure, who forgets to pass
Through water that looks like the word isinglass.

Rhu Mor

Gannets fall like the heads of tridents,
bombarding the green silk water
off Rhu Mor. A salt seabeast of a timber
pushes its long snout
up on the sand, where a seal,
struggling in the straightwaistcoat of its own skin,
violently shuffles towards the frayed wave,
the spinning sandgrains, the caves of green.

I sit in the dunes – the wind
has moulded the sand in pastry frills
and cornices: flights of grass
are stuck in it – their smooth shafts shiver
with trickling drops of light.

Space opens and from the heart of the matter
sheds a descending grace that makes,
for a moment, that naked thing, being,
a thing to understand.

I look out from it
at the grave and simple elements
gathered round a barrage of gannets
whose detonations
explode the green into white.

Incident

I look across the table and think
(fiery with love)
Ask me, go on, ask me
to do something impossible,
something freakishly useless,
something unimaginable and inimitable

like making a finger break into blossom
or walking for half an hour in twenty minutes
or remembering tomorrow.

I will you to ask it.
But all you say is
Will you give me a cigarette?
And I smile and,
returning to the marvellous world
of possibility,
I give you one
with a hand that trembles
with a human trembling.

Among the Talk and the Laughter

Why does he fall silent?
Why does that terrible, sad look
tell he has gone away?

He has died too often.
And something has been said
that makes him aware of the bodies
floating face downwards
in his mind.

Sounds of the Day

When a clatter came,
it was horses crossing the ford.
When the air creaked, it was
a lapwing seeing us off the premises
of its private marsh. A snuffling puff
ten yards from the boat was the tide blocking and
unblocking a hole in a rock.
When the black drums rolled, it was water
falling sixty feet into itself.

When the door
scraped shut, it was the end
of all the sounds there are.

You left me
beside the quietest fire in the world.

I thought I was hurt in my pride only,
forgetting that,
when you plunge your hand in freezing water,
you feel
a bangle of ice round your wrist
before the whole hand goes numb.

The Piper in the Dark

The far notes were blaeberries – bubbles
of blue blood in the dark.
They clustered towards me, turning red.

Cold constellations in your mind
(those nights in days, those days in nights)
clustered towards me, shivering with oracles.

The piper in the dark walked
under his own flourish – delicately inserting
the punctuation and pointing of gracenotes.

He passed me with an eyebrow greeting. The night
slowly withdrew him till one last
blue berry fainted into the darkness.

But the oracles remained, coldly promising
an exhilaration of abundances, a precision
of the art you are, of your delicate gracenotes.

Antique Shop Window

Spearsman of molasses, shepherdess
cut from a sugar block, rings with
varicose stones – all
on a one-legged table perched
on a birdclaw.

And your face in the glass and
my face in the glass, and the real world
behind us translated before us
into dim images, there
– so that the spearsman crouches
on a bird-legged table in
a busy street and the shepherdess runs
through head after head after head
and who can tell
if your face is haunted by the world
or the world by your face?

Look left at the birds stitched
still in their singing, at the sword
half drawn from the scabbard – look left,
more left, to me, this side of the window,
a two-legged, man-legged cabinet
of antique feelings, all of them
genuine.

Hotel Room, 12th Floor

This morning I watched from here
a helicopter skirting like a damaged insect
the Empire State Building, that
jumbo size dentist's drill, and landing
on the roof of the PanAm skyscraper.
But now midnight has come in
from foreign places. Its uncivilized darkness
is shot at by a million lit windows, all
ups and acrosses.

But midnight is not
so easily defeated. I lie in bed, between
a radio and a television set, and hear
the wildest of warwhoops continually ululating through
the glittering canyons and gulches –
police cars and ambulances racing
to the broken bones, the harsh screaming
from coldwater flats, the blood
glazed on sidewalks.

The frontier is never
somewhere else. And no stockades
can keep the midnight out.

Heron

It stands in water, wrapped in heron. It makes
An absolute exclusion of everything else
By disappearing in itself, yet is the presence
Of hidden pools and secret, reedy lakes.
It twirls small fish from the bright water flakes.

(Glog goes the small fish down.) With lifted head
And no shoulders at all, it periscopes round –
Steps, like an aunty, forward – gives itself shoulders
And vanishes, a shilling in a pound,
Making no sight as other things make no sound.

Until, releasing its own spring, it fills
The air with heron, finds its height and goes,
A spear between two clouds. A cliff receives it
And it is gargoyle. All around it hills
Stand in the sea; wind from a brown sail spills.

Goat

The goat, with amber dumb-bells in his eyes,
The blasé lecher, inquisitive as sin,
White sarcasm walking, proof against surprise,

The nothing like him goat, goat-in-itself,
Idea of goatishness made flesh, pure essence
In idle masquerade on a rocky shelf –

Hangs upside down from lushest grass to twitch
A shrivelled blade from the cliff's barren chest,
And holds the grass well lost; the narrowest niche

Is frame for the devil's face; the steepest thatch
Of barn or byre is pavement to his foot;
The last, loved rose a prisoner to his snatch;

And the man in his man-ness, passing, feels suddenly
Hypocrite found out, hearing behind him that
Vulgar vibrato, thin derisive me-eh.

Truth for Comfort

So much effect, and yet so much a cause –
Where things crowd close she is a space to be in:
She makes a marvel where a nowhere was.

Now she's not here I make this nowhere one
That's her effect and it becomes a marvel
To be more marvellous when her journey's done.

Ideas can perch on a nerve and sing.
I listen to their singing and discover
That she can share herself with everything.

This chair, this jug, this picture speak as her,
If in a muted way. Is that so crazy?
My singing mind says No, and I concur.

And is this lies for comfort? She won't know
(Who could not be the cause of lies) for comfort's
What I won't need, until she has to go.

Walking to Inveruplan

Glowing with answers in the aromatic dark,
I walk, so wise,
Under the final problem of lit skies.

I reach the bridge, where the road turns north to Stoer,
And there perch me
Under the final problem of a tree.

I'm in my Li Po mood. I've half a mind
To sit and drink
Until the moon, that's just arisen, should sink.

The whisky's good, it constellates. How wise
Can a man be,
I think, inside that final problem, me.

If you are short of answers, I've got them all
As clear as day . . .
I blink at the moon and put the bottle away

And then walk on (for there are miles to go
And friends to meet)
Above the final problem of my feet.

Names

In that shallow water
swim extraordinary little fish
with extraordinary names
they don't know they've been given –
rock goby, lumpsucker, father lasher.

I sit among sea lavender and see it. Easy
to point and say buckthorn,
tamarisk, purple rocket.
But they no more know these names
than I know who named them.

I know your name and who named you.
But you have selves as secret from me
as blenny or butterfish.
I sit by you and see you
with eyes ignorant as a glasswort
and I name you and name you
and wonder how it is
that the weight of your name, the most ponderable
thing I know, should raise up
my thoughts
from one shallow pool to
another where
we move always sideways to each other, like
a velvet fiddler and a porcelain crab.

A Man in My Position

Hear my words carefully.
Some are spoken
not by me, but
by a man in my position.

What right has he
to use my mouth? I hate him
when he touches you
the wrong way.

Yet he loves you also,
this appalling stranger
who makes windows of my eyes.
You see him looking out.

Until he dies
of my love for you
hear my words carefully –
for who is talking now?

Sleeping Compartment

I don't like this, being carried sideways
through the night. I feel wrong and helpless – like
a timber broadside in a fast stream.

Such a way of moving may suit
that odd snake the sidewinder
in Arizona: but not me in Perthshire.

I feel at rightangles to everything,
a crossgrain in existence. – It scrapes
the top of my head, and my footsoles.

To forget outside is no help either –
then I become a blockage
in the long gut of the train.

I try to think I'm a through-the-looking-glass
mountaineer bivouacked
on a ledge five feet high.

It's no good. I go sidelong.
I rock sideways. . . . I draw in my feet
to let Aviemore pass.

Waiting to Notice

I sprawl among seapinks - a statue
fallen from the ruins
of the air into
the twentieth century - and think:
A crowd of fancies is not so easily come by
as you suppose. They have to happen
like weather, or a migration, or a haystack
going up in flames all on its own
half-way through some time or other.
When they happen, the mind alerts itself -
it's as if this landscape were suddenly
to become aware
of the existence of its own elements -
possessive rock, possessing
only itself: huge lumbering sea -
that fat-fingered lacemaker who,
by sitting on shells, gives them
their shapes: mountains
reaching half-way to somewhere or other:
and heather and grass and me
and a gull, as usual
tuning his bagpipe
and not going on to the tune.

Things there to be noticed.

It takes a sunshaft
to reveal the motes in the air. I wait
for that weather, that sunshaft
to show in the dark room of my mind
that invisible dancing, that

wayward and ceaseless activity, and I bend
my stone arm up till the hawk
hovering over the hayfield
perches fluttering
on my wrist.

In My Mind

I go back ways to hurl rooftops
into that furze-blazing sunset.

I stare at water
frilling a stone, flexing a muscle.

Down sidestreets I sniff
cats in passages, old soup and

in one hot room
the fierce smell of hyacinths.

From the tops of spires
I lasso two counties in an eyeblink

and break my ears with a jukebox
in a frowsy cellar.

I am an honorary citizen
of these landscapes and a City Father

of this city. I walk
through its walls and burn

as traffic lights. It is all
lines on my hand.

But I turn away
from that terrible cul de sac.

I turn away from
the smiling house there

and the room in it
with green blinds drawn

and a bed with a bed lamp shedding
its kind light down

on a dead hand
and a book fallen from it.

Go-Between

Out of a night
that felt like a grape's skin
an owl's voice shuddered.
Out of the running
blackness of a river pool
a white salmon unplugged
itself and fell back
in a smash of light.
Out of the throat of
a duck flying over,
delicate, Japanese
on the blue plate of the sky,
came a croaking grunt,
catarrhal and fat-living.
Out of your never
averted face, come
classical admonitions
of the finality of form
and the untrespassable regions
beyond it. I go
poaching there and come
back with news of
an owl's hoot, exploding
salmon and the profound eructations
from the flat nose of
a delicate duck.

Since I am your convert
and true believer, I have
to enlarge the admonitions
of your never averted face

to include these wild regions
where the lunacy of form
is normal and caricature
impossible. Am I bringing
your news to them or their news
to you? Am I evangelizing
the duck or you? – For how can a man
breathe hymns to the Lord
with one lung and hymns to the devil
with the other?

Power Dive

He spent a fortune on architects and builders.
He signed tickertapes of cheques for furniture,
carpets, paintings, filmstar beds. He surrounded the house
with plantations and parterres, hahas and gazebos.
And in the right place, the properest place
at last he saw completed a swimmingpool
that glittered like ancient Rome.

It was just before he hit the water
in his first dive that he glimpsed
the triangular fin cutting the surface.

Assisi

The dwarf with his hands on backwards
sat, slumped like a half-filled sack
on tiny twisted legs from which
sawdust might run,
outside the three tiers of churches built
in honour of St Francis, brother
of the poor, talker with birds, over whom
he had the advantage
of not being dead yet.

A priest explained
how clever it was of Giotto
to make his frescoes tell stories
that would reveal to the illiterate the goodness
of God and the suffering
of His Son. I understood
the explanation and
the cleverness.

A rush of tourists, clucking contentedly,
fluttered after him as he scattered
the grain of the Word. It was they who had passed
the ruined temple outside, whose eyes
wept pus, whose back was higher
than his head, whose lopsided mouth
said *Grazie* in a voice as sweet
as a child's when she speaks to her mother
or a bird's when it spoke
to St Francis.

The Root of It

On the rug by the fire
a stack of vocabulary rose up, confidently
piling adjectives and nouns and
tiny muscular verbs, storey by storey,
till they reached
almost to the ceiling. The word at the bottom
was love.

I rushed from the room. I
didn't believe it. Feverishly
I turned over the pages of the dictionary
to find the blank spaces
they had left behind them – and there they were,
terrible as eyesockets.

What am I to do? What
am I to do? For I know
that tall stack would collapse,
every word would fly back and fill
those terrible spaces,
if I could snatch that word
from the bottom of the pile – if
I could learn again
the meaning of love.

Visiting Hour

The hospital smell
combs my nostrils
as they go bobbing along
green and yellow corridors.

What seems a corpse
is trundled into a lift and vanishes
heavenward.

I will not feel, I will not
feel, until
I have to.

Nurses walk lightly, swiftly,
here and up and down and there,
their slender waists miraculously
carrying their burden
of so much pain, so
many deaths, their eyes
still clear after
so many farewells.

Ward 7. She lies
in a white cave of forgetfulness.
A withered hand
trembles on its stalk. Eyes move
behind eyelids too heavy
to raise. Into an arm wasted
of colour a glass fang is fixed,
not guzzling but giving.
And between her and me

distance shrinks till there is none left
but the distance of pain that neither she nor I
can cross.

She smiles a little at this
black figure in her white cave
who clumsily rises
in the round swimming waves of a bell
and dizzily goes off, growing fainter,
not smaller, leaving behind only
books that will not be read
and fruitless fruits.

Bluestocking

Anything I say
she judiciously considers with
quotations and references.
What weight is anything I say
when in the other scalepan she puts
St Augustine and Chomsky?

Such a length of learning!
I can no more approach her
than one bookend
can approach the other.

Even her tears,
I think savagely,
will drop from each eye in pairs,
quoting her nose.

And yet she's pretty . . .
If only I could bluepencil
this bluestocking
and get down to
the original script.

To Make a Poem

He determined
before the day was out he'd shoot
the ventriloquist
in the syllable tree.

He stalked the voice
along ditches of nouns
and across
the verb river.

He lay still
in a camouflage of white.
He striped himself
with blue.

Then bang! his blunderbuss
belched
making a snow
of green syllables.

He slept that night
in a downdrift of voices
each one uttering
words of love.

Aunt Julia

Aunt Julia spoke Gaelic
very loud and very fast.
I could not answer her –
I could not understand her.

She wore men's boots
when she wore any.
– I can see her strong foot,
stained with peat,
paddling the treadle of the spinningwheel
while her right hand drew yarn
marvellously out of the air.

Hers was the only house
where I've lain at night
in the absolute darkness
of a box bed, listening to
crickets being friendly.

She was buckets
and water flouncing into them.
She was winds pouring wetly
round house-ends.
She was brown eggs, black skirts
and a keeper of threepenny bits
in a teapot.

Aunt Julia spoke Gaelic
very loud and very fast.
By the time I had learned
a little, she lay

silenced in the absolute black
of a sandy grave
at Luskentyre.
But I hear her still, welcoming me
with a seagull's voice
across a hundred yards
of peatscrapes and lazybeds
and getting angry, getting angry
with so many questions
unanswered.

Memorial

Everywhere she dies. Everywhere I go she dies.
No sunrise, no city square, no lurking beautiful mountain
but has her death in it.
The silence of her dying sounds through
the carousel of language, it's a web
on which laughter stitches itself. How can my hand
clasp another's when between them
is that thick death, that intolerable distance?

She grieves for my grief. Dying, she tells me
that bird dives from the sun, that fish
leaps into it. No crocus is carved more gently
than the way her dying
shapes my mind. – But I hear, too,
the other words,
black words that make the sound
of soundlessness, that name the nowhere
she is continuously going into. In every minute
I grow into marvellous things and
die towards her.

Ever since she died
she can't stop dying. She makes me
her elegy. I am a walking masterpiece,
a true fiction,
of the ugliness of death.
I am her sad music.

Excuse

You make me a weather
that erodes time
and decorates its gulches and ledges
with childish flowers, till it looks like
a slightly tipsy old lady
enjoying herself.

I play on space
like a concertina –
I stretch it and shrink it, playing
the tune of you.

When I think
that the mountain remains
and there's an end to the tune,
do you wonder I attack time
with increasing ferocity? Do you wonder
I play that tune
louder and louder?

Excess is not enough –
though, being a reasonable man,
I sigh and
put up with it.

Wild Oats

Every day I see from my window
pigeons, up on a roof ledge – the males
are wobbling gyroscopes of lust.

Last week a stranger joined them, a snowwhite
pouting fantail,
Mae West in the Women's Guild.
What becks, what croo-croos, what
demented pirouetting, what a lack
of moustaches to stroke.

The females – no need to be one of them
to know
exactly what they were thinking – pretended
she wasn't there
and went dowdily on with whatever
pigeons do when they're knitting.

Centre of Centres

To call the pier a centre
I sit in a centre –
of cloud-stuffs, water lispings, a huge
charge of light and men doing things on boats
that result in fish. Yet I am, too, a centre
of roundabouts and No Entries, libraries,
streets full of cafés and the prickly stink
of burnt petrol:
an imposition of two circles
from different geometries
where a coincident stream refuses to be
the street it's coincident with
and a skyscraper offers no ledge
to twirling, laborious ravens.

Where's my binocular vision now?
I see like a bird or a fish,
a boat with one eye a bus with the other,
a crofter left a traffic warden right:
a supermarket ghosts up
from the shallows of Loch Fewin
and round the foot of Suilven
go red deer and taxis.

The *Golden Emblem* seethes in, sidles
and with a friendly nudge stables herself
beside the *Valhalla*. Round my head
she releases a flicker of names that come out of
geography but emerge from myth –
Muckle Flugga, Taransay, Sule Skerry,
the Old Man of Hoy.

– Though I know
she's been no farther off than Coigach Point
she has ringed her nets in the imagination
as well as the Minch
and brings ashore a cargo
the fishbuyers won't bid for.
– So, with my other eye, from my other centre
I look at Edinburgh's High Street and a film
starts unwinding, spool on spool,
of caddies and clan chiefs, lords
and layabouts – in a broad daylight's midnight
desperate men
pull themselves up the Castle Rock –
a scabbard clinks: whispers curse
the scaling ladder.

So where's my binocular vision again?
How many geometries are there
with how many circles
to be a centre of?
As though a man, alive in his imagination,
trips on this stone and stumbles
on the field of the Battle of the Braes or, walking
to Murrayfield, is one of a crowd
moving in silence
to the execution of Montrose.

I name myself I name this place I say
I am here; and the immediacies
of the flesh and of the reports
of its five senses (I come to them)
make their customary
miraculous declaration, from which
all else falls away

in natural recession. The landscapes
and histories of memory
disappear in a yellow basket
rising from the hold of the *Golden Emblem* and swooping
ashore, towsy with fishtails
(gray haddock, falseface skate, flounders
with wrong eyes – they slide into the shallow boxes
with a slip with a slither, watched by me
and by herring gulls and blackbacks that stroll
the fringe of the crowd like policemen,
like pickpockets).

Who would guess
the thorn in the rosetree, the scandalous life
of Professor Schmaltz, the grunt
of a puffin? The argument from design
has as many flaws in it as there are
unpredictables
in the design.

I think of a man who talks as if trees were
virtuosities of wood, as if water
were liquid mechanisms built for holding up
swans. He speaks as if winds were
recordings of a master wind and not
unexampled discourses, as if birds
were spools of song that
they unwind.

What sort of apprentice sorcerer is he
whose inventions
have got out of hand? – For he forgets
the intrusion of the comic (see that sun, strolling over,
lordly magnifico, with a wig of cloud

slipping over one ear) – and of the tragic:
that whimsical water
lullabying in the sun can clench its fist
on the timbers it cradles.

In mid-air a gull, peering down, bowed
between its wings,
unbows itself and cackles,
trips over the cackle and floats on;
and a baby boat
comically staggering across the bay
stops for a rest in the dead centre
of teeming unpredictables.

Grassblade cathedral hero
strawberry jam pot – each
is a centre of
innumerable circles. I sit in mine
enriched by geometries
that make a plenum of more
than the three dimensions.
I sit and stare at them
with a multiple eye.

Battlefield Near Inverness

Only dead bodies lie here,
for dreams are not to be buried.
You can't keep down with a stone
the stink of loyalty and honour
that still poison the air
with all the corpses they've made
since the air rotted at Culloden.

No Fairy Tale

To prove it
I gathered around her like trees.
In some of them
an owl snored
or a squirrel made a feather boa
of his tail.
The snow balanced on every twig
sparkled greenishly
in the mild sunlight.

Who could place
behind that bush a bandit,
under that tree a staring wolf?
Who could suppose
a lie hissing in the brake?
Who in such glades and shades
could invent wrong music
or a word noosed from a branch
or a mantrap number?

So she smiled, and walked through those trees
into
my terrible cottage
where I lay waiting for her
with my what big eyes,
with my what big teeth.

Rock Below Suilven

Ten feet high: plumpuddinged
with glassy pebbles colourful as flowers.
A trickle of spring water
sponges the grass it's bedded in.

The bankrupt air breathes to itself.
Small water ripples sigh
of a homeless desolation. Deer traverse
their beautiful, derelict landscape.

No use to say to that rich rock
Open Sesame. Its jewels are clenched
in the past where buried people
insult the ground with their spent lives.

Ace of Spades

Years that were hedgerows,
enclosing, each, its neat twelve acres,
waft and waver – they are
brilliant mists that make new things
by sidlings, by interpenetrations.
They fit my panning eye
with irresponsible zoom lenses
that suck third February 1954
into a today's close-up
and rush yesterday backwards
into Lilliput.

It's as if I were cutting the cards I was given
by the gambler
who always wins.
I turn them over
more and more fearfully
in case I see staring up at me
the black centre of brightness.

GEORGE MACKAY BROWN

from THE STORM (1954)

The Storm

What blinding storm there was! How it
Flashed with a leap and lance of nails,
    Lurching, O suddenly
    Over the lambing hills,

Hounding me there! With sobbing lungs
I reeled past kirk and alehouse
    And the thousand candles
    Of gorse round my mother's yard,

And down the sand shot out my skiff
Into the long green jaws, while deep
    In summer's sultry throat
    Dry thunder stammered.

Swiftly the sail drew me over
The snarling Sound, scudding before
    The heraldic clouds now
    Rampant all around.

The sea – organ and harps – wailed miserere;
Swung me in fluent valleys, poised
    On icy yielding peaks
    Hissing spume, until

Rousay before me, the stout mast
Snapped, billowing down helpless sail.
    What evil joy the storm
    Seized us! plunged and spun!

And flung us, skiff and man (wave-crossed, God-lost)
On a rasp of rock! . . . The shore breakers,
    Stained chancel lights,
    Cluster of mellow bells,

Crossed hands, scent of holy water ...
The storm danced over all that night,
    Loud with demons, but I
    Safe in Brother Colm's cell.

Next morning in tranced sunshine
The corn lay squashed on every hill;
    Tang and tern were strewn
    Among highest pastures.

I tell you this, my son: after
That Godsent storm, I find peace here
    These many years with
    The Gray Monks of Eynhallow.

The Exile

So, blinded with Love
He tried to blunder
Out of that field
Of floods and thunder.

The frontiers were closed.
At every gate
The sworded pitiless
Angels wait.

There's no retreat.
The path mounts higher
And every summit
Fringed with fire.

The night is blind,
Dark winds, dark rains:
But now his blood
Pours through his veins,

His hammer heart
Thuds in his breast
'What Love devises,
That is best,'

And he would not turn,
Though the further side
Dowered his days
With fame and pride.

What though his feet
Are hurt and bare?
Love walks with him
In the menacing air.

The frontiers sealed;
His foot on the stone;
And low in the East
The gash of dawn.

Song: 'Further than Hoy'

Further than Hoy
the mermaids whisper
through ivory shells
a-babble with vowels

Further than history
the legends thicken,
the buried broken
vases and columns

Further than fame
are fleas and visions,
the hermit's cave
under the mountain

Further than song
the hushed awakening
of sylvan children,
the harp unstroked

Further than death
your feet will come
to the forest, black forest
where Love walks, alone.

from LOAVES AND FISHES (1959)

That Night in Troy

The wind was fire; the streets hot funnels; women
Went trailing lamentation round the walls
Searching for father or husband or son who lay
Churned in the rubble.
                              Far off, where the sky
Curved like a claw upon the tawny plain
A casual smudge showed where the spoilers marched
To rouse their ships from ten years' arid slumber
(Each prow was buried deep in fleeting seapinks).

Over the carnival hill the stars trooped out.
The moon got up and walked across the sky
And laid bright fingers on the harp of Troy,
Smashed by an alien hoof.
                              In one poor hovel
(So poor the enemy had passed it by
With a sneer and a spit) a girl spoke certain words
To the blind god of sheaf and shoal and cluster –
The haggard bundle whining in her arms
A redder conqueror than Agamemnon.
    Among his prisms a philosopher
(He was dying not of swords but of the brightening
Blizzard of age) said to the smiling lad
Who chafed his hands and fired his thoughtful clay:
'What was that uproar in the streets at noon?
It sounded like swift cataracts of thaw
In mountain valleys, winter's last lustration
Before the ploughman chants across the glebe
His liturgy of spring, turning a page
With every patient furrow'. . . .
                              On a dark plinth

(Its marble general toppled) Corydon crouched,
Glowing with agony for three tall brothers
Broken beneath the wheels.
                                        A girl from the temple
Where lust all day had knit
Soldiers and vestals into sweating knots
Under the images whose eyes were vacant,
Stumbled upon him there.
                                        A crystal finger
Tuned an invisible string.
                                        With their first kiss
A ten years' vogue was out, and Paris died.
Since one unbroken string can lure dead stones
Into a solemn architectural dance
And lead in order through the finished gate
The horse, the wheel, the god, the golden corn,
They sealed a resurrection for the city.

Ulysses' prow over the formal waves
Led him the long way home. He turned his head
And saw far back, far back, the burning town.
He thought for an idle moment that it looked
Like a red rooted rose, symbol of love.
The spray went glancing past. He could not tell
If the drop that stung his cheek was bitter sea
Or the sudden image of a woman weaving.

GEORGE MACKAY BROWN

The Masque of Bread

What answer would he give, now he had reached
The Inquisitor's door, down seventy hungry streets,
Each poorer than the last, the last a slum
Rambling like nightmare round his penitent feet?

The Inquisitor's door? The walls were all blank there,
But a white bakehouse with a little arch
And a creaking sign. . . . Against the fragrant doorpost
He clung, like drifted snow, while the shuttered oven
Opened on hills of harvest sun and corn.

The loaf the bakers laid on the long shelf
Was bearded, thewed, goldcrusted like a god.
Each drew a mask over his gentle eyes
– Masks of the wolf, the boar, the hawk, the reaper –
And in mock passion clawed the bread.
                                        But he
Who stood between the cold Plough and the embers
In the door of death, knew that this masquerade
Was a pure seeking past a swarm of symbols,
The millwheel, sun, and scythe, and ox, and harrow,
Station by station to that simple act
Of terror or love, that broke the hill apart.
But what stood there – an Angel with a sword
Or Grinning Rags – astride the kindled seed?

He knelt in the doorway. Still no question came
And still he knew no answer.

                                The bread lay broken,

Fragmented light and song.

                        When the first steeple
Shook out petals of morning, long bright robes
Circled in order round the man that died.

Port of Venus

The holy earl, his kestrel pilgrimage
Hardly begun, furled sails in a strange port
Out of the kick of the gale and the salt siege,
And all the sailors called for a night's sport

With foreign girls and ale, eyeing their lord,
Ignorant of what sanctities he planned –
Unlock the city granaries with his sword,
Or lay a cold mouth on the prince's hand

To get fresh corn aboard his famished ships.
The square was mild with doves. The elders came
And led this hawkwing, in a barnyard choir,
To greet their prince, a girl with snooded hair
And shy cold breasts. They trembled as their lips
Welded holy and carnal in one flame.

The Stranger

One night he stayed with us
(Said the tall proud woman)
One night in our poor house
And then mounted his mare
And clattered thankless forth.
I've thought him ever since
A great one of the earth
– A poet or a prince –
Touched with unlucky fire.

That night when I was laid
(Sang the milking girl)
Sound in my box bed
He broke upon my rest
And in the deep midnight
Turned that first cruel pain
Into a wild delight
That buds and flowers again
When his child seeks my breast.

What was he but a tink
(Cried the obstinate man)
All rags, blether, and stink?
Yet when he slouched through that door
Begging a slice of bread
And a drop of ale in a glass
The old wife bowed her head,
And a throb went through our lass
As though an angel stood there.

Hamnavoe

My father passed with his penny letters
Through closes opening and shutting like legends
    When barbarous with gulls
    Hamnavoe's morning broke

On the salt and tar steps. Herring boats,
Puffing red sails, the tillers
    Of cold horizons, leaned
    Down the gull-gaunt tide

And threw dark nets on sudden silver harvests.
A stallion at the sweet fountain
    Dredged water, and touched
    Fire from steel-kissed cobbles.

Hard on noon four bearded merchants
Past the pipe-spitting pier-head strolled,
    Holy with greed, chanting
    Their slow grave jargon.

A tinker keened like a tartan gull
At cuithe-hung doors. A crofter lass
    Trudged through the lavish dung
    In a dream of cornstalks and milk.

In 'The Arctic Whaler' three blue elbows fell,
Regular as waves, from beards spumy with porter,
    Till the amber day ebbed out
    To its black dregs.

The boats drove furrows homeward, like ploughmen
In blizzards of gulls. Gaelic fisher girls
    Flashed knife and dirge
    Over drifts of herring,

And boys with penny wands lured gleams
From the tangled veins of the flood. Houses went blind
    Up one steep close, for a
    Grief by the shrouded nets.

The kirk, in a gale of psalms, went heaving through
A tumult of roofs, freighted for heaven. And lovers
    Unblessed by steeples, lay under
    The buttered bannock of the moon.

He quenched his lantern, leaving the last door.
Because of his gay poverty that kept
    My seapink innocence
    From the worm and black wind;

And because, under equality's sun,
All things wear now to a common soiling,
    In the fire of images
    Gladly I put my hand
    To save that day for him.

The Death Bird

(i)

Pen, take no wings on you
But trail black scars across the page
Calamitously to record
For all grocers to be
That Knarston, justice of the peace, is dead,
Washed home by the last cold wave.

Or rather, on Wednesday,
The clock in his skull rang 'Time'
And startled him under the hill.
The lark was silent.
                              A bird
Winged with fivers,
Sovereigns birling in the throat,
Shrieked across his dying.

In the play of The Death Bird
All the actors came out well
Except for the hero
Who had spasms of stage fright.

        In the end, all the same,
        They smothered him in flowers
        And bore him off, shoulder high.

(ii)

A week later Peero died
Feet pointing at the stars,
Thoroughly soused

In holy beer and dew.
They gave him back to God
    Without a flower or a tear.

But over the corn
A lark sang, wildly cheering
    Peero's sweet translation
    From ratflesh to light
(Thought Halcro, Peero's neighbour, his tongue
Sacramental with malt, his eyes
Grieving like angels. He stuck
A haloed candle in the wine bottle
Peero drained last week.)

Unfortunately, according to counter and pew,
    According to books of the month,
    According to singing reels and smoking guns,
    According to umbrellas and spats
Halcro is a damned liar
And his three tears
Are not angels
Nor saints of sorrow
But a drunken leak.

      (Not for all under the hill
      Over the hill a lark stammers
      Abracadabra of joy.)

Chapel Between Cornfield and Shore

Above the ebb, that gray uprooted wall
Was arch and chancel, choir and sanctuary,
A solid round of stone and ritual.
Knox brought all down in his wild hogmanay.

The wave turns round. New ceremonies will thrust
From the thrawn acre where those good stones bleed
Like corn compelling sun and rain and dust
After the crucifixion of the seed.

Restore to that maimed rockpool, when the flood
Sounds all her lucent strings, its ocean dance;
And let the bronze bell nod and cry above
Ploughshare and creel; and sieged with hungry sins
A fisher priest offer our spindrift bread
For the hooked hands and harrowed heart of Love.

from THE YEAR OF THE WHALE
(1965)

Horseman and Seals

On the green holm they built their church.
There were three arches.
They walked to the village across the ebb.
From this house they got milk.
A farmer cut and carted their peats.
On their rock
Fishermen left a basket of mouthing silver.
They brought the gifts of heaven
To the new children and the suffering shapes.
They returned to the island
And mixed their bell with the seven sounds of the sea.
Eight times a day
They murmured their psalms in that gray place.

A horseman stood at the shore, his feet in seaweed.
He could not cross over.
The sea lay round the holm, a bright girdle.
His voice scattered in the vastness
Though from shore to shore pierced cries of gull and petrel.
What did the horseman want?
Perhaps an old man in the parish was sick,
Or he wanted a blessing on his ship,
Or he wished to argue a point in theology.
From shore to shore they blessed him.
They trooped under the arch for nones.
After the psalms the horseman was still there,
Patient in the seaweed.
The sea shone higher round the skerry.
And the abbot said, 'Cormac, you are the carpenter,
A blessed occupation,
And tomorrow you will beg some boards and nails

And you will build a little boat,
So that we do not need to keep horsemen waiting on the
   other shore
Who are in need of God' . . .

And while the boat was building under the crag
Paul gathered whelks.
From the cold triangular pools he gathered handfuls
And put them in his basket.
He sang *Dominus Pascit Me*, gathering whelks.
Twenty seals lay on the skerry.
They turned their faces towards the psalm.
The brother sang for them also,
For the seals with their beautiful gentle old men's faces.
Then the ebb subtracted one sound
From the seven-fold harmony of ocean.
The tide lay slack, between ebb and flowing, a slipped girdle.
Paul gathered whelks and sang
Till the flood set in from the west, with a sound like harps,
And one by one the seals entered the new water.

Trout Fisher

Semphill, his hat stuck full of hooks
  Sits drinking ale
    Among the English fishing visitors,
  Probes in detail
      Their faults in casting, reeling, selection of flies.
'Never,' he urges, 'do what it says in the books.'
      Then they, obscurely wise,
    Abandon by the loch their dripping oars
  And hang their throttled tarnish on the scale.

'Forgive me, every speckled trout,'
  Says Semphill then,
    'And every swan and eider on these waters.
  Certain strange men
      Taking advantage of my poverty
Have wheedled all my subtle loch-craft out
      So that their butchery
    Seem fine technique in the ear of wives and
      daughters.
  And I betray the loch for a white coin.'

Hamnavoe Market

They drove to the Market with ringing pockets.

Folsten found a girl
Who put wounds on his face and throat,
Small and diagonal, like red doves.

Johnston stood beside the barrel.
All day he stood there.
He woke in a ditch, his mouth full of ashes.

Grieve bought a balloon and a goldfish.
He swung through the air.
He fired shotguns, rolled pennies, ate sweet fog from a stick.

Heddle was at the Market also.
I know nothing of his activities.
He is and always was a quiet man.

Garson fought three rounds with a negro boxer,
And received thirty shillings,
Much applause, and an eye loaded with thunder.

Where did they find Flett?
They found him in a brazen circle,
All flame and blood, a new Salvationist.

A gypsy saw in the hand of Halcro
Great strolling herds, harvests, a proud woman.
He wintered in the poorhouse.

They drove home from the Market under the stars
Except for Johnston
Who lay in a ditch, his mouth full of dying fires.

Weather Bestiary

Rain

    The unicorn melts through his prism. Sodden hooves
    Have deluged the corn with light.

Wind

    A fisherman wets his finger. The eyelash
    Of the gray stallion brushes his blood with cold.

Sun

    A hard summer. The month I sat at the rock
    One fish rose, belly up, a dead gleam.

Thunder

    Corn, lobster, fleece hotly harvested – now
    That whale stranded on the blue rock!

Frost

    Stiff windless flower, hearse-blossom,
    Show us the brightness of blood, stars, apples.

Fog

    The sun-dipped isle was suddenly a sheep
    Lost and stupid, a dense wet tremulous fleece.

Snow

    Autumn, a moulted parrot, eyes with terror
    This weird white cat. It drifts the rose-bush under.

The Sailor, the Old Woman, and the Girl

'Have you any help,' cried the young sailor
Pulling against the tide,
'Have you any spell or herb to mend
This new pain in my side?'

The old woman gathering whelks
Raised her fierce gray head.
'The best cure in the world for that
Is, take her to your bed.

If watchdogs howl, there's two good places
To end a lover's moans –
The alehouse with its lamp and barrel,
The kirkyard with its stones.

Or use the black worm of the mind.
Think, when she leans up close
And all the lurings of Delilah
Break open like a rose

Against your eyes and throat and mouth,
That I am lying there,
Time's first lover stark as a thorn
In a white winter air.'

The girl sang from another shore
And the tranced oars beat on,
And the old woman's fingers went
Like roots through the gray stone.

Harald, the Agnostic Ale-Drinking Shepherd, Enemy of Ploughmen and Elders and All the Dancing Sons of Barleycorn, Walks over the Sabbath Hill to the Shearing

Two bells go pealing through my age,
Two mad majestic criers.
One celebrates the pastured saints,
One descants on hell fires.
They storm at me with trembling mouths
And both of them are liars.

The barman had a little bell
That swayed my soul to peace
At ten last night.
               When the mad horns
Raged in the barley lees,
From lip to bottom of my glass
Clung a shining fleece.

The Seven Houses: In Memory of John F. Kennedy

Man, you are at the first door.
The woman receives you.
The woman takes you in.
With joy she takes you into her long hall.
The nine candles are burning.
Here with reptile and fish and beast
You dance in silence.
Here is the table with the first food.
This is the House of the Womb.

Man, you are the second door.
A woman receives you.
With brief hands she holds you.
She delivers you into time,
Into light and darkness,
Into sound and silence and a new dance.
From an outer spring
The natural water comes to your mouth.
Also on your head
A man lays seven bright drops.
This is the House of Birth.

Man, you are at the third door.
A tree in a gray courtyard.
Here the animals dare not enter.
The tree is loaded with apples.
Three women stand at the tree,
The bare bitter bloody tree.
With oil and cloths they stand at the tortured tree.
This is the House of Man.

Man, you are at the fourth door.
Ploughman, merchant, engineer
Cross in a busy street.
On the seven oceans beyond
The ships sail on,
The peoples exchanging oil and wheat and music.
The cornstalk is tall in the field.
Through those yellow tides, that peace,
One woman comes,
On her shoulder a tall jar of untasted wine.
This is the House of Corn and Grape.

Man, you are at the fifth door.
The woman has brought you to her gate.
You have drunk her wine.
She has washed your hands at the threshold.
Now she prepares a bed.
Under the seven stars you watch and wait.
Inside, flames twist and untwist their hair.
This is the House of Love.

Man, you are at the sixth door.
The enemies with sculptured faces,
Stiffly they dance
About the disordered dangerous board.
The broken pitcher spills its oil.
Dark at the wall
The harp is a tangle of strings.
The hungry sit at a narrow table
And the Golden Man
Summons another beast from the flames.
The negro hangs on his tree.
At the sixth wall
In growing darkness, you lit one lamp.
This is the House of Policy.

Man, you are at the last door.
Three small mad venomous birds
Define in your skull
A new territory of silence.
The darkness staggered.
Seventy thousand ordered days
Lay ravelled in the arms of a woman.
In a concord of grief
The enemies laid aside their masks,
And later resumed them
For epitaph, platitude, anger.
What they say is of small importance.
Through the arrogance of atom and planet
May the lamp still burn
And bread be broken at the tables of poor men
(The heads bowed
And the sweet shape of the dove at the door.)
This is the House of History.

from A SPELL FOR GREEN CORN
(1970)

The Ballad of John Barleycorn

As I was ploughing in my field
The hungriest furrow ever torn
Followed my plough and she did cry
'Have you seen my mate John Barleycorn?'

Says I, 'Has he got a yellow beard?
Is he always whispering night and morn?
Does he up and dance when the wind is high?'
Says she, 'That's my John Barleycorn.

One day they took a cruel knife
(O, I am weary and forlorn!)
They struck him at his golden prayer.
They killed my priest, John Barleycorn.

They laid him on a wooden cart,
Of all his summer glory shorn,
And threshers broke with stick and stave
The shining bones of Barleycorn.

The miller's stone went round and round.
They rolled him underneath with scorn.
The miller filled a hundred sacks
With the crushed pride of Barleycorn.

A baker came by and bought his dust.
That was a madman, I'll be sworn.
He burned my hero in a rage
Of twisting flames, John Barleycorn.

A brewer came by and stole his heart.
Alas, that ever I was born!
He thrust it in a brimming vat
And drowned my dear John Barleycorn.

And now I travel narrow roads,
My hungry feet are dark and worn,
But no one in this winter world
Has seen my dancer Barleycorn.' . . .

I took a bannock from my bag.
Lord, how her empty mouth did yawn!
Says I, 'Your starving days are done
For here's your lost John Barleycorn.'

I took a bottle from my pouch,
I poured out whisky in a horn.
Says I, 'Put by your grief, for here
Is the merry blood of Barleycorn.'

She ate, she drank, she laughed, she danced,
And home with me she did return.
By candle light in my old straw bed
She wept no more for Barleycorn.

from FISHERMEN WITH PLOUGHS
(1971)

Building the Ship

'A dove must fold your seed from dragon flame.'

That blind rune stabbed the sea tribe.
Fishermen sought a bird in the mountains.

Their axes kept them that year from the dragon.
Logs throttled a mountain torrent.
A goatherd gaped on the lumbering tons.

Saws shrieked, sputtered, were sharpened, sang.
Dunes were pale with strewment of boards.
Seaward a keel was laid.
Sprang from that spine a vibrant cluster of ribs.

Forge and anvil begot a host of rivets.
Shavings, blond hair of excited children,
Curled from the combing adzes.
A woodman died of a rotten nail.
(Njal found, near falcons, an urn for his fires.)

Men daylaboured, were dappled with lanterns.
They beat design on the thwart timbers.
Loomed a dry dove from June leafage.
That bird would unlock the horizon westwards.
Now visit, dragon, a blank shore.
Tar pots chuckled like negroes over the fires.

Moons, seven fish, swam through that labour.
A summer whirled its golden hoof.
'Trees for this doveflight,' cried Norn among the looms,
'Would blacken the coast with yawls.'
(Njal brought Gudrun down, a cold jar.)
'We sup sawdust broth,' sang the workmen.
Thorkeld drove the hammers. Their hands bled.

The Fight with the Dragon

Thorkeld stood that night between Dragon and Dove.
Horn, hoofbeat, triumph of the blind mouth.
The moon was a huge cinder.
'Our guest is generous with his flames,' said Thorkeld.

Thorkeld stood in a smoulder of nets.
His cold mouth touched the sword.
'Into their fires, long sharp fish,' he said,
'See if this Dragon will relish you.'
The Dove was astir in the trestles.
At the shore the Dragon tasted the bronze fish.

Thorkeld turned. He splintered the stable door.
The mares were a row of charred skulls.
'Thunder', he coaxed a garnet eye.
The stallion reared at the stars like a red wave.

Thorkeld unbolted the door of the women.
He plucked Gudrun from a hundred shrieks.
Hoof-fast Njal bore his manseed wombfurled waveward.

Thorkeld a blacksmith, the Dragon a blown forge.

Thorkeld stood at the altar of the god Balder.
He strewed that stone with dragon scales.
The village burned around like oil barrels.
'Now on a new shore,' said Thorkeld,
'This folk can give the star shoal a better name.'
The dog Bran licked his charcoal hand.
The sun rose. Thorkeld gave himself to the sea.

Thorkeld brought to the blind westering Dove
A body charted with twelve wounds.

The Statue in the Hills

Croft Women

Our Lady of Cornstalks
Our Lady of the Flail
Our Lady of Winnowing
Our Lady of Querns
Our Lady of the Oven
Blue Tabernacle
Our Lady of the Five Loaves
            Take the ploughmen home
                sober from the alehouse.

Fishermen

Our Lady of the Boat
Our Lady of Oil and Salt
Our Lady of the Inshore
Our Lady of the Silver Dancers
Our Lady of Nets
Our Lady of the Atlantic
Star of the Sea
            May cuithe and codling
                hang in the chimney smoke

Shepherds

Our Lady of Lent
Our Lady of the Last Snow
Our Lady of Muirburn
Fold of the Agnus Dei
Our Lady of Quiet Waters
Our Lady of Daffodils
Our Lady of April
            Guard the labour of
                thirty-five ewes.

Tinkers

> Our Lady of Vagabonds
> Our Lady of Fishbone and Crust
> Our Lady of Ditch Fires
> (It was a long road that,
> Bethlehem to Golgotha
> And you at the end Pieta, quiet chalice)
> Our Lady of Pilgrims
>> We have this last can to
>> sell at the doors.

Washer Women

> Our Lady of Wind and Sun
> Our Lady of the Pool
> (As we scrub shirts for ploughmen
> Make clean our hearts, Lady)
> Clother of the Child Christ
> Preparer of linen for the unborn and the dead
> Our Lady Immaculate
>> That these shirts be dry
>> by dewfall.

Death Watchers

> Our Lady of the Last Oil
> Our Lady of Silence
> Our Lady of Two Candles
> Mater Dolorosa
> Our Lady of Dark Saturday
> Stone of these stones
> Our Lady of the Garden
>> Pray for old Sara cold
>> as roots.

The Croft at Night

        Our Lady of Dark Ploughs
        Our Lady of Furled Boats
        Our Lady of Kneeling Oxen
        (And their breath was warm on thy hand one
            winter)

        On an old pillow, blessing
        On the cradle, blessing
        On those laid together in love, blessing

        Our Lady of Perpetual Vigil.

A Winter Bride

The three fishermen said to Jess of The Shore
'A wave took Jock
Between The Kist and The Sneuk.
We couldn't get him, however we placed the boat.
With all that drag and clutch and swell
He has maybe one in a hundred chances.'
They left some mouthing cuithes in the door.
She had stood in this threshold, fire and innocence,
A winter bride.
Now she laid off her workaday shawl.
She put on the black.
(Girl and widow across a drowned wife
Laid wondering neck on neck.)
She took the soundless choir of fish
And a sharp knife
And went the hundred steps to the pool in the rock.
Give us this day our daily bread
She swilled and cut
And laid psalms and blessings on her dish.

In the bay the waves pursued their indifferent dances.

A Warped Boat

As one would say, lighting an evening pipe
At a banked fire,
'Barley will soon be ripe.
Ale should be sweet in the mouth this year
With all that rain in May, though the seedtime was dry'. . . .
So Willag, before the *Merle* turned over
Rose from the rowlocks
And remarked to the open mouths on the shore,
'Drive old Bess, that fence-breaker, from the oats
Back to her patch of clover.
Yes, Breck can have my horse for his five goats.
And Jeannie is wrong again.
She raged by all that was holy I'd drown and die
In steepings of malt.
A fine evening it was for going to the sillocks.
But men,
It's a coarse drink at the end of a day, this salt.'

His sea boots filled, and Willag said no more.

Foldings

What they fold, what the shepherds fold
Is this, in March
A mothering huddle.

The crofter's trade a hoarding, folding, burnishing
Of seed from snow.

What the fishermen fold is this,
A sklinter of haddocks
From the breached Atlantic banks.

What the women fold
Are torn nets, a stretch of yarn from the loom,
Sheaf after sheaf of August oats,
In the cupboard cheese and honey and ale and bread,
Shapes in the womb,
Night long as a shroud when the twelve boats
Are drifting lights in the west
And the ebb ravels itself in rock and sand.

A winter bride is ravished with plough and seed
And finds at last
The crag where mother and widow enfolded stand.

Love Letter

To Mistress Madeline Corston, widow
At Quoy, parish of Voes, in the time of hay:

The old woman sat in her chair, mouth agape
At the end of April.
There were buttercups in a jar in the window.

The floor is not a blue mirror now
And the table has flies and bits of crust on it.

Also the lamp glass is broken.

I have the shop at the end of the house
With sugar, tea, tobacco, paraffin
And, for whisperers, a cup of whisky.

There is a cow, a lady of butter, in the long silk grass
And seven sheep on Moorfea.

The croft girls are too young.
Nothing but giggles, lipstick, and gramophone records.

Walk over the hill Friday evening.
Enter without knocking
If you see one red rose in the window.

The Laird

Once it was spring with me
  Stone shield and sundial
Lily and lamb in the Lenten grass;
The ribs of crag and tree
      Resurrecting with birds;
In the mouths of passing crofter and fisher lass
Shy folded words.

Then one tall summer came
  Stone shield and sundial
The year of gun and rod and hawk;
The hills all purple flame;
      The burn supple with trout;
Candle-light, claret, kisses, witty talk,
Crinoline, flute.

Autumn, all russet, fell
  Stone shield and sundial
I wore the golden harvest beard.
I folded my people well
      In shield and fable.
Elders and councillors hung upon my word
At the long table.

Now winter shrinks the heart
  Stone shield and sundial
I'd quit this withered heraldry
To drive with Jock in his cart
      To the hill for peat,
Or seed a field, or from clutches of sea
Save a torn net.

Ikey the Tinker Crosses the Ward Hill to the Spanish Wreck

Because of the Spanish wreck I tackled the hill.
I heard of the apples,
Winekegs, mermaids, green silk bale upon bale.

My belly hollowed with hunger on the hill.
From Black Meg's patch
I plucked the loan of a curl of raw kail.

We both wore patches, me and that harvest hill.
Past kirk and croft,
Past school and smithy I went, past manse and mill.

On the black height of the hill
I lay like a god.
Far below the crofters came and went, and suffered, and
    did my will.

I wrung a rabbit and fire from the flank of the hill.
In slow dark circles
Another robber of barrows slouched, the kestrel.

Corn and nets on the downslope of the hill.
The girl at Reumin
Called off her dog, poured me a bowl of ale.

I found no silk or brandy. A bit of a sail
Covered a shape at the rock.
Round it the women set up their terrible wail.

The Scarecrow in the Schoolmaster's Oats

Hail, Mister Snowman. Farewell,
Gray consumptive.

Rain. A sleeve dripping.
Broken mirrors all about me.

A thrush laid eggs in my pocket.
My April coat was one long rapture.

I push back green spume, yellow breakers,
King Canute.

One morning I handled infinite gold,
King Midas.

I do not trust Ikey the tinker.
He has a worse coat.

A Hogmanay sun the colour of whisky
Seeps through my rags.
I am – what you guess – King Barleycorn.

Dead Fires

At Burnmouth the door hangs from a broken hinge
And the fire is out.

The windows of Shore empty sockets
And the hearth coldness.

At Bunertoon the small drains are choked.
Thrushes sing in the chimney.

Stars shine through the roofbeams of Scar.
No flame is needed
To warm ghost and nettle and rat.

Greenhill is sunk in a new bog.
No kneeling woman
Blows red wind through squares of ancient turf.

The Moss is a tumble of stones.
That one black stone
Is the stone where the hearth fire was rooted.

In Crawnest the sunken hearth
Was an altar for priests of legend,
Old seamen from the clippers with silken beards.

The three-toed pot at the wall of Park
Is lost to woman's cunning.
A slow fire of rust eats the cold iron.

The sheep drift through Reumin all winter.
Sheep and snow
Blanch fleetingly the black stone.

From that sacred stone the children of the valley
Drifted lovewards
And out of labour to the lettered kirkyard stone.

The fire beat like a heart in each house
From the first cornerstone
Till they led through a sagging lintel the last old one.

The poor and the good fires are all quenched.
Now, cold angel, keep the valley
From the bedlam and cinders of A Black Pentecost.

from NEW POEMS (1971)

THE MASQUE OF PRINCES

Sea Jarl

> Arkol the skald mingled these
> words with harp strokes
> at the Earl's Hall at
> Orphir in Orkney in the
> Yuletide of 1015.

Our salt march ended before the city.
The king said, 'Their roofs are tall.'
We closed the five roads into the city.
They threw down stones from the wall.
Bones were broken, a skull, twelve ribs.
We commandeered fields round the city
And cattle, barns, horses, women, wells.
They threw down fire from the wall.
The wind was red.
Roofbeams hissed in the Seine.
We circled the wall with dice and wineskin.
The city rotted slowly
Like a spotted corpse in a charnel.
They threw down insult and curse
But that hurt no one,
The men from the fjords are not sensitive.
Armand the spy reported
Now they were eating rats in the city
And fungus that creeps between stone.
The merchants (said Armand) were poor as the students
And the priests distracted
With shrivings, anointings, requiems.

When the wind lay towards the city
We turned the sputtering ox on the spit.
On the fortieth day the stones were disordered
And Ragnar stood in the gate.
Tapestry. Vats. Opal. Nakedness. Ashes.
The harp was silent. I drew my fingers through silver.
We stayed in the city seven days,
Then dragged carts to the ships at the mouth of the river.
We waited two nights for a wind.
I put the siege in a set of formal verses.
The skippers did not praise that poem.
(This is for blacksmiths and poachers.)
We arrived in Jutland in time for the spring sowing
With a cargo of silver, corn, foreign rats.

Lord of the Mirrors

A dance Bernard of Ventadour
made, with masks and
lutes and ladies, for
the investiture of
Philip Count of Narbonne
in April 1130

The prince questioned his ancient shield

Lord, the first quartering sheweth
A skull, a sheaf of corn, a mask
(Your bread is uttered on long cold throats)

Prince, the second quartering sheweth
A skull, a sword, a mask
(Your soldiers gleam at the five gates)

Sire, the third quartering sheweth
A skull, a harp, a mask
(Poets stain your parchment with nightingale notes)

Man, the fourth quartering is blank
    'Between skull and mask
    This face, a bright withering flower'

A breath, surge of cloud,
    through the bronze mirror.

*

The new prince goes among roses, cupids, peacocks

Beast, what is love?
Phallus, rut, spasm

Peasant, what is love?
Plough, furrow, seed

Priest, what is love?
Prophecy, event, ritual

Lord, what is love?
Lys, and daunce, and viol

Man, what is love?

> On the garden pool breezes, a
> caul of sackcloth.

*

The new prince kneels at a rood, scarlet and black

Man, where have you been this loud April day?
I followed the hounds to a kill.

Man, what have you done with the royal stag?
Five wounds I bore to a ruined hall.

Man, who received that sacrifice?
A lady, stricken and still.

Man, was there food in that barn?
The rat had devoured the earth gold.

> On nothing they
> thundered, the heavy
> stones in the mill.

Man, what lamp in the rafters?
One star that pierced like a nail.

Man, was there fire on that hearth?
Breathings of ox and ass. The woman cried
   in the straw. Then night laid
   a shroud on the hill.

That vigil done,
The rood was rose 'of ravissement and ruth'.
      *
Now, Mask-and-Skull, rear high among the trumpets!

Prince in the Heather

> The bard Alasdair MacNiall
> made this in Barra
> the day after the true
> prince left Scotland
> for France, 1746

Who would have thought the land we grew in, our mother
Would turn on us like a harlot?
The rock where the stag stood at dawn,
His antlers a proud script against the sky,
Gave us no shelter.
That April morning the long black rain
Bogged our feet down
But it did not douche the terrible fire of the English,
Their spewings of flame.
(I think it will rain a long time at Culloden
And steel rot under the stone.)
Who would have thought our own people,
Men of our tongue and lineage,
Would make one wall that day with barbarians?
We prayed our endless mountain tracks
Would baffle the hunters
But the armies marched like doom on the one road
To the one graveyard.
Who would have thought for a moment
But that our leaders had wisdom,
Men skilled in the ancient rites and duties of warfare?
Tinkers from a ditch
Would have directed the lines better that morning.
Casually the cannonball burst those ribs,
Removed that leg.

They harried us like rats from a granary,
A fury worse than dogs.
A great shining thing is gone forever from the glens.
Sheep drift through the halls of the chief and his lady.
The white rose is withered.
Now grandsons of hunter, fisherman, bard
Must turn high courtesy to unction,
A manner and a speech to please the Saxons,
A thing never known before.
Who would have thought our prince, that hero,
While we plucked broken steel from the forge of our valour,
Would take to the screes, a frightened stag?

White Emperor

A troop of irregular soldiers
led by a woman sing these
choruses on the road near
Ekaterinburg, March 1918

What are you, skeleton with the bayonet?
The Ploughman

What are you, skeleton with rifle and bullets?
The Sower

What are you, skeleton dragging a field gun?
The Harrower

What are you, scarecrow with the knife?
The Reaper

What are you, scarecrow with stones?
The Miller

What are you, shadow among the ashes?
The Baker

*

Unmasked, the Little Father and his children
    Drift on. The sky is red.
Five winters now he has given us blood and snow
    For our daily bread.

Now in the fifth winter the rat is king
    Of furrow and mill.
That golden mask has worn you, Little Father
    Down to the skull.

Mane and sabre whirl against the sunset.
    Those princes turn
And fade in the snow. From Omsk to Warsaw, this
        starfall,
    The Russias burn.
           *

Who called us brothers of ox and mule?
Peasants we were,
Children of The White King.

Who calls us skeletons, rags, shadows?
Soldiers we are,
Comrades of The Red One.

We are the people. Forge and field are ours.
I am Natasha.
I measure the sun with lucent eyes.

King of Kings

The inn-keeper at Bethlehem
writes secret letters to the
Third Secretary (Security)
at the door marked with
dolphins in the fifth street
north from Temple and
Dove-market

Came the first day of the week five guardsmen, Greeks. No
sleep in the village for their choruses. Their lamp still
burned at sunrise. One broken jar. Rachel's scent was in
the sergeant's sheets. Came a troop of merchants, solemn
men, with currants in their satchels, they were up and
gone early, on four camels, southward. *Who will pay for the
jar?* I said to the guardsmen. *Caesar,* said a corporal. *Rachel,*
said the sergeant, *she broke it. And anyway,* said a guards-
man, *the drink was bad.* God keep me from guests like them.
It was this summer's wine, the leaven still moving in it, a
little cloud. The Chian and Syrian are for silk purses.

*

These passed through my door yesterday— Jude and Abrim
and Saul, farmers. Jude had sold an ox at the mart. *A fire in
the back room, a lamp, dice, a skin of wine,* said Jude. An
Egyptian with scars on his face, he left the northbound
camel train, he ate barley cakes and fish and was most
courteous and laid Ethiop coins on the table. Then
Abrim's wife, crying under the stars, *Where is Abrim? He
hasn't come home, the bull is in the marsh, his children are hungry,
he is with Rachel, I know it, she will have his last penny.* The
Egyptian leaned his knife-marked face from his window.

The wife of Abrim took one look at him then turned and wrapped her in night and silence. The Egyptian looked from the stars to a chart he had on the sill. He made comparisons, measurements.

*

The Egyptian is still here. He asks me after breakfast, could he get a guide as far as the border? *I have certain persons to meet in the desert,* said he. In the afternoon he left with Simon, donkey by donkey, a muted going. This was the sole guest today, except for a rout of farm servants and shepherds who lay about the barrel like piglets at the teats of a sow, and sung and uttered filth and (two of them) David a ploughman and Amos a shepherd roared about the alleys after Rachel. They came back with bleeding faces, separate and silent, after midnight. Such scum.

*

My brain is reeling from a press of faces! I had no warning of this. First came two bureaucrats, a Parthian and a Cypriot, bearing Caesar's seal, and a boy with them. *Your best room,* said the Cypriot. (For these chitbearers you get paid a half-year later.) Then came a little company of clerks with scrolls and ledgers and wax and moneybags and a wolf on a chain. They set up benches in the courtyard. Then – O my God – by every road north and south they came, a horde of hook-noses, hillmen, yokels, they swarmed about the doors, come to pay some tribal tax, filthy thirsty goats. *We'll sleep on the roof,* said some. And others, *Provide beer and bread, never mind blankets.* And Rachel shining among them like a fish in a pool. A measured clash of bronze: a column of soldiers possessed the village. And the lieutenant, *I commandeer six rooms. There are no six rooms,* I said. *I commandeer the whole inn,* he said. The Cypriot stood in the door. *I commandeer the whole inn except for the rooms of Caesar's civil servants,* said the lieutenant. *And the room of the chief clerk,* said the Cypriot, *and the room of my hound, and the room of Eros.* (Eros is their catamite.) Never was such a day in this place. The till rattled, I don't deny it, a hundred throats gargled the new wine. Ditches between here and Hebron will be well dunged.

*

The skin is full of blots and scratchings and bad spellings. Put it down to this – my trade is lighting fires, listening, going with chamber pots, whispering, heating cold porridge; not scrivener's work. Know however, the yokels are back in the hills, poor as goats after the taxes and the revelry. Out of Rachel's room all morning small sweet snores. The clerks are balancing figures in their ledgers, melting wax in small flames. The bureaucrats are playing at chess in their room and sipping the old Chian. Eros, like Rachel, sleeps. The soldiers polish their greaves and drink and throw dice; two of them, bare and bronze-knuckled and bloodied, boxed in the sand at noon. There came a man and a woman from the north to pay the tax, very late, and wanted a room. This was after dark. I had one place, ox and ass kept it warm with winter breathings. I gave the man a lantern.

*

The tax-men have gone, a clash of bronze on one side, a wedge of steel on the other, the Parthian on horseback before, the Cypriot on horseback behind, the wolf chained to the money cart, Eros carried by two black men in a silk chair, swaying aloft like a tulip. The first star brought the shepherds. *The soldiers have drunk all the wine,* I said. Amos stood well back in the shadows. *You,* I said, *Amos, stay*

*outside, never come back. I bar you from this place. You and your
punch-ups and your pewkings.* I said sweetly to the others,
The Romans have dried the barrel. The shepherds drifted on
past me. One carried a new white winter lamb.

*

Most secret and urgent. Aaron will bring this on horseback,
direct from inn to palace, helter-skelter, a shower of
hooves and stars. The negro with the cut cheeks has come
back, and with him an Indian and one from very far east
with eyes like grass-blades. In the first light they seemed
like revellers masked and weary from a carnival. They had
men servants with them, heavy baggage on the mules,
bales and jars. I lit fires, put out sweet water, spread woven
blankets over linen. They went about the village all day
with questing eyes. I poked among the baggage – ingots,
cruets, chalices, tiaras, candlesticks, swords, thuribles,
swathe upon swathe of heavy green silk, emeralds cold as
ice. They came back late. They wrote their names in the
guest book, steep square letters like Hindu temples, like
ships of Cathay. I cannot read it, I have torn out the page
for your perusal. *Please,* I said, *to enter places of origin.* Coal
Face murmured, *The broken kingdoms of this world,* and
wrote in the book. Nothing in the room for a while but
shadows and flutters. *Also enter,* I said, *the nature of your
business. You understand, the imperial government requires this.*
Bronze Face said, *Bearers of precious gifts.* Nothing again –
one star that hung a web of glimmers and shadows
about the chamber. *Blessings given to men in the beginning,*
he went on at last, *that have been wrongly spent, on pomp,
wars, usury, whoredoms, vainglory: ill-used heavenly gifts. We
no longer know what to do with these mysteries. Our thrones
are broken. We have brought the old treasures here by difficult
ways. We are looking for the hands that first gave them, in the*

ancient original kingdom. We will offer them back again. Let them shine now in the ceremonies of the poor. I lit a cluster of seven candles at the wall. *But first we must find the kingdom'* said Daffodil Face, smiling. *Perhaps this kingdom does not exist. Perhaps we found it and did not recognize it. Perhaps it is hidden so deep in birth and love and death that we will never find it. If so, we will leave our skulls in the desert. We do not know where we should go from here. Perhaps the kingdom is a very simple thing.* I kept my hands clasped and my head to one side. *Landlord,* said Coal Face, *your guests tonight are poor lost cold hungry kings. What have you got for us in your cellar?* I informed them that their rooms were ready. I said that I had bread with honey and currants and dates in it, baked that same morning. I mentioned Rachel. I said also my inn was famous for wines, in keg or skin or flagon. I hoped the gentlemen would enjoy their stay. It was cold, I said, for the time of year. They did not move. The night was a sack of coal with one diamond in it. I turned to the door.

MORE ABOUT PENGUINS

Penguinews, which appears every month, contains details of all the new books issued by Penguins as they are published. From time to time it is supplemented by *Penguins in Print*, which is a complete list of all available books published by Penguins. (There are well over three thousand of these.)

A specimen copy of *Penguinews* will be sent to you free on request, and you can become a subscriber for the price of the postage. For a year's issues (including the complete lists) please send 30p if you live in the United Kingdom, or 60p if you live elsewhere. Just write to Dept EP, Penguin Books Ltd, Harmondsworth, Middlesex, enclosing a cheque or postal order, and your name will be added to the mailing list.

Note: *Penguinews* and *Penguins in Print* are not available in the U.S.A. or Canada

PENGUIN MODERN POETS

*Not for sale in the U.S.A.
†Not for sale in the U.S.A. or Canada